WHO WE ARE

WHO WE ARE

A LONG AND MAGICAL JOURNEY

Colleen Costello

BALBOA.
PRESS

A DIVISION OF HAY HOUSE

Balboa Press books may be ordered through booksellers or by contacting:

Balboa Press
A Division of Hay House
1663 Liberty Drive
Bloomington, IN 47403
www.balboapress.com
1-(877) 407-4847

ISBN: 978-1-4525-4116-7 (sc)
ISBN: 978-1-4525-4118-1 (hc)
ISBN: 978-1-4525-4117-4 (e)

Library of Congress Control Number: 2011918419

Because of the dynamic nature of the Internet, any web addresses or links contained in this book may have changed since publication and may no longer be valid. The views expressed in this work are solely those of the author and do not necessarily reflect the views of the publisher, and the publisher hereby disclaims any responsibility for them.

The author of this book does not dispense medical advice or prescribe the use of any technique as a form of treatment for physical, emotional, or medical problems without the advice of a physician, either directly or indirectly. The intent of the author is only to offer information of a general nature to help you in your quest for emotional and spiritual well-being. In the event you use any of the information in this book for yourself, which is your constitutional right, the author and the publisher assume no responsibility for your actions.

Any people depicted in stock imagery provided by Thinkstock are models, and such images are being used for illustrative purposes only.
Certain stock imagery © Thinkstock.

Printed in the United States of America

Balboa Press rev. date: 10/24/2011

Contents

Acknowledgements and gratitude

Thank you

Father God, Archangel Michael and Light Beings

My dear family for their love and my sister her wisdom

Balboa Press for their kind help

With honorable mention of Loren D. Adams, Jr. for the cover image of his original oil painting: "The Naacal Temple of the Pristine Wilderness"

"The Naacal Temple of the Pristine Wilderness" original oil painting was commissioned in 1987 by (The Red Rocker) Sammy Hagar.

Thank you Father God and Angels for everyone who has been a part of my life

With love and light

Chapter 1

Journey through the galaxies and dimensions

We have been such travellers. We have travelled through space and time and seen the most magnificent sights and beauty along the way. We have been everywhere and done everything though we have forgotten the brilliance and just how beautiful we are. We have forgotten where we came from but we will remember this again soon, as we always do.

We are love, we are perfect and we are like Angels. Father God has created us and our Creator is perfect. Our soul is very beautiful and we have a beautiful light that desires to shine brightly. We are all one with all and that includes being one with God. Because we are all one, if we hurt our brother then we hurt ourselves and if we hurt ourselves then we hurt our brother and so we should remember to always be kind to ourselves.

We are Divine little bright lights and we have come here from the Heart of our Creator to live on Gaia, Great Mother Earth for a while so that our soul has the opportunity to experience spiritual life while at the same time be in a body and to remember who we are and our connections to our Creator. Shortly we will have the possibility to bring Heaven down to Earth once again with the new Golden Age as was in the previous Golden Ages.

The perfect Golden Age has been and gone more than once and it is returning again and all of great Mother Earth will be once again beautiful and full of bright shining light. Also the everlasting life in the solar systems has been and gone more than once.

We will be able to understand all this one day. It is like a circle, everything goes around like the seasons, everything is forever changing and will go on changing, round and round, coming and going and we will venture on.

We have travelled long and far and many aeons ago some of us were there for the first Golden Age called the Polarian Age which was then quite magnificent and perfect with trees, flowers, much beauty and located in the Arctic Circle. We were crystalline in structure at that time and we were very much connected to our Creator Father God.

Long after this period there came the Hyperborean Golden Age which again was perfect with beautiful plants and trees, and though still crystalline in our form we then became slightly dense and still close to our Creator.

There were other stages throughout these ages though this is mainly about the Golden Ages and also the Golden Age to come when we return to the beauty and perfection as it had been in the Land of Mu during golden times.

The third and wondrous Golden Age was called Lemuria, where we were then able to express emotions as later on in Lemuria the birthing process started. However in the early times of Lemuria, then called Mu, more new souls came and some took the beautiful Holy Innocents to the crystal clear waters so as to adjust and later on to join together with beautiful Gaia Mother Earth.

They had come down surrounded in bubbles or spheres of bright light, and with them they brought all they needed from our Creator for their journey and they went into the clear blue lakes staying for a while as they blended with the beautiful sea creatures such as the dolphins until the time came when they were used to the environment of Gaia.

Long ago and later on we were separated from our soul family, from our twin flames when we went to the different places in the universe and some of us came here to the great Mother Earth Gaia.

The magnificent crystalline beings as we were then were made into tiny little pieces so that we could travel to these places which were then more dense than the beauty of the light from where we had come. We could not come down to the density as we were then, as this would not be possible because of our bright light. The light was far too bright for the lower dimensions and so we refracted into little souls or little bright lights.

During our time here on Gaia we have fallen down many times, we have been sad and lonely and yet we have managed to get up, to dust ourselves down and venture on. We have been hurt and we have been loved and we have been made well and sparkling once more. We have experienced the extremes, the ups and downs and everything possible during our journey. We are very special indeed and soon in the future we will remember just how beautiful and special we really are. We have been everywhere and done everything and we are such wonderful beings. You could call us all little souls or Divine little sparks of light and we are all so very special.

Many of us have a part of these beautiful Angels in our own heart soul. We are from the line of the Angels and every one of us is as important as the next person; we are just a different aspect of our Creator God though we have forgotten all this while in our earthly vehicle.

There is only one truth and that is the truth which is our own because we all resonate on a different vibration, and if we live from our hearts rather than our heads and follow our intuitions and feelings, then we will find our own truth which will feel right and comfortable with us. A great teacher once said, to go within.

Many ages ago, two little bright lights called Mariah and Jo came from our Father Creator's heart centre, they journeyed down from the Great Central Sun, on and on down through the dimensions and magnificent galaxies and many star systems.

There were many other little bright lights which you could also call little souls and they were all very special because they all came from Father God.

The sky was painted beautiful deep blue with billions of sparkling bright stars glowing like diamonds. The moon and the colours we could not imagine at present with our limited human minds. Little, compared to the knowledge of our little bright light. There were bright shiny colours like rainbows of light and sometimes colourful lights would pass across or down the sky making beautiful patterns, expanding up and out, brilliant bright lights like searchlights.

The little bright lights or young souls wanted to see and experience everything as a little child does. They wanted to travel around and discover and so they came from our Creator's heart, down through all the different dimensions and beautiful galaxies and planets and some stayed for a while before venturing on.

It was joyous to be able to do this time after time throughout the ages and could continue to do so forever, travelling to different star systems and galaxies and then back to Father God from where they first came.

There was also a very special planet further away with colours of blue white and green. She was just a little planet, Mother Earth Gaia and she was different to the other planets as on this planet the people would have a human body as well as their bright little light. Lady Gaia is name of the over soul of Great Mother Earth, as Mother Earth has a soul just the same as we have a soul.

Yes, there was something unusual going on with this beautiful planet Gaia, for the people on earth would be able to help create through their thoughts, they would have free will and make their own decisions and would also be able experience their emotions and feelings while in a human body.

These beautiful little Divine lights would have a human body and they would experience life in the time of a beautiful Golden Age when everything was perfect and in harmony.

Gaia was a most beautiful and shining planet with wonderful great deep oceans of azure and turquoise colours, more vivid than you could imagine and as the sun shone on her waters they looked like white sparkling diamonds and on the shore line the waves gently glistened like white lace.

The grass was emerald green and felt like velvet. The leaves on the trees sometimes changing to yellow or red at different seasons; gentle winds whistling through the trees playing their beautiful music and streams gently flowing over the rocks and stones, finding their way through the forests and on to the rivers out to the sea.

Yes, this was looking very exciting and interesting to some of the little bright lights.

Then they also saw the high peaked mountains, and lakes that mirrored the tall trees making a pretty picture in the clear water. There were little animals running up the trees chasing each other having fun and excitement and squeaking in delight. Bright coloured fish in the water, jumping out sometimes, and simply beautiful were the dolphins rising and falling elegantly over the surface of the waters with their happy smiley faces.

The little souls also noticed the birds flying to and fro between the trees, chasing each other, catching up and tweeting with joy.

Many of the little bright lights could see that Gaia was a delight and so decided that they would like to share in this.

Some were so intrigued by this little planet Lady Gaia that they felt they would like to live through the wonder of life in a human body and to be able to know what it feels like to have emotions and feelings, to laugh and dance in a body, to have free will and to be able to make choices, to learn and to experience all they could along the way.

. . . . This is the story of Mariah and Jo, two little bright lights from the heart of Father God and their journey through the Golden Ages and the 'Winds of Change' about to come, forever the winds of change.

They were twin flames and they wanted to experience life on earth in the beginning times. They experienced some of the wonderful Golden Ages together and Lemuria and Atlantis which were like heaven on earth. They had left and then returned again to the times when the earth had sunk very low in the third dimension and some people's lights were not shining very brightly and people had become greedy and controlling and had forgotten how to love as they did before they came to earth and in the earlier times of life on Gaia.

Mariah and Jo had sometimes journeyed to the same places together though sometimes they would be in other galaxies or dimensions at different times but being twin flames they were always together, as everyone is. They may have forgotten each other for a short time while in the human body as at those times sometimes it is easy to forget where we have come from and the true beauty of our souls.

That is because they could become bogged down with their earthly thoughts and worries but deep down they knew that they were part of all that is—they were one—as a feeling deep down made them remember this and they had a yearning to be together again.

Mariah and Jo were deeply connected as we all are. They were together many times that they could remember and during those times they laughed and danced and played with beautiful beings and creatures along their way, also experiencing the heights and the depths. They had experienced and learnt so much while in their life on earth and also other experiences in other dimensions.

Beautiful Mother Earth Gaia

They were both now on a higher dimension above the earth and could see the beauty and wonders of Mother Earth but as they were such very young little souls they hesitated as to which step they should take next. Should they stay where they were in the world of spirit, or should they become a part of the beautiful material world?

Maria and Jo could see the amazement of life on earth and loved it all. They were such enquiring little souls and so they decided to unite their awareness with the bodies of Gaia's friendly little dolphins. These wonderful creatures played happily together enjoying the smooth feel of the water while making beautiful music of nature's sounds. They were full of fun and joy.

After a while though Mariah and Jo did desire to have a change as they now felt that they would like to know a lot more about life.

So the next thing they did was blend their little bright light with the essence of other beautiful aspects of Mother Nature, the wind and the magnificent trees and plants.

Then Mariah and Jo joined with the birds from the cherry tree and flew high and could taste the juice from the fruits and flowers as the birds did. They laughed and sang and made wonderful chirping noises and looked down at the beautiful scenery as they glided overhead, free and in harmony.

The two little souls later wondered if there was more for them to experience as Gaia was such a big and wondrous planet.

Many ages further on, Mariah and Jo began to notice that on the land of the breathtaking Great Mother Earth there walked living beings. These beings were loving and exquisite.

Mariah and Jo wondered if they would be able to experience and learn more about Great Mother Earth and about themselves by joining these beings. Yes, they thought that this would be a wonderful idea, so they decided to join their awareness with these beautiful beings and this was such a magnificent journey for them.

However, this time Mariah and Jo had stayed on earth in their human vessel for such a very long time, there was so much for them to do. They were like little children who wanted to experience everything but now because so much time had passed they could no longer remove their little bright lights on their own as they could earlier. It was so much more different now.

There was now the death process partly because all the little bright lights had now a sense of not being truly at one with all and with our Father God as they had been originally; they had developed fear and so this had come about over time.

Because so much time had passed they now had to stay in their human bodies until their natural life time here on Gaia had completed and it was time for them to leave the earth plane. Then the little bright lights which were eternal and never really die were free to go back to the realm from where they had last come. They soon learnt that we never die, we just change form.

The magnificent Angel of Light

Mariah and Jo also loved being in this other realm, this other dimension in a higher realm. The beings there were loving and beautiful and it was peaceful and colourful. They noticed a tiny brilliant light in the distance; it slowly came towards them as it got bigger. This Being was so bright with light he almost dazzled the little souls. He had bright light the colour of pure diamonds expanding all around and out from him.

They wondered was this an Angel. They could not see clearly with the shining light, though they both felt very loved and comfortable in His presence. The Angel sat on a big flat rock surrounded by emerald green grass while a pretty bird and a unicorn watched curiously nearby.

The wings of the tiny bird were sky blue and white and it circled inquisitively around Mariah and Jo before flying and watching from a nearby tree. The Unicorn came over to the twin flames and put its head towards their faces, each in turn. The eyes on the Unicorn were bright and loving and kind. She was pure white with a shining light coming from her forehead shaped like you could imagine on unicorn's forehead, a shining bright horn of light.

There were magnificent old trees that seemed to look ancient and very wise, with roots spread out for a long way across the ground as well as beneath the earth. Their unusual branches coming all the way down from the top to the earth almost like arms. Mariah and Jo felt the urge to run up and cuddle these big giant like trees; also flowers of the kind the little souls had forgotten existed, they were very large and brightly coloured and as well had more bright colours coming from each leaf and tree like a rainbow.

Everything was surrounded by rainbow colours. Jo reminded Mariah that was the aura; they would remember that on earth sometimes people could see these extra colours and sometimes people could not.

They loved being in the presence of the Angel who shone so brightly. This beautiful being of light told them that he would care for them and look after them very well.

He listened to all their stories which they were so excited to talk about, they were getting all their words jumbled as trying to get so much in each sentence.

'After being on earth for a long time I had forgotten where I had come from. I had forgotten that I had come down through all those beautiful stars and galaxies and before that from our Creator's heart. It was like a veil had been placed over my memory and I was only aware of what was happening on earth at that time,' said Jo.

'I could not remember that we are all one and that we are magnificent beings, but I did remember somewhere inside of me that if I hurt another person I would be hurting myself,' Mariah said with a sad tone in her voice.

'I did have some wonderful experiences and learnt much, though sometimes I was sad. Sometimes it was very exciting and joyful and sometimes it was painful. On looking back I feel there is more that I could find out and discover or do differently; so much more to do,' continued Mariah.

They both said to the brilliant Angel that they would like to go back to Gaia again and learn and to know more about what it means to be both a spiritual and a human being, even though it might not always be easy to remember the beautiful beings that they really are or where they had come from.

Jo and Mariah knew that they would because they wanted to learn to shine brightly and to become knowing and wise and to do a better job this time than they did last time.

'I want to remember who I really am, when I go back to Gaia. I don't want to forget the bright little light that I am; I want to remember and to help others on Gaia to remember also. When I am on Gaia I want to remember about love and Father God,' said Jo.

Returning to beautiful Lemuria

Mariah and Jo went off together to enjoy very many more unusual and exciting experiences. They knew that if they should forget where they had come from or forget that they were not alone, they would always be connected to our

11

Creator Father God and that after a time something inside them would remind them who they both were and where they had come from.

They would remember in those times when their minds were still and not worrying about everything they would hear the guidance. Perhaps it would be their guardian or a beautiful Angel nudging them to remember who they really are. Perhaps it would be Father God reminding them. But they realised now that they would always have help and guidance.

'I hope that if I do forget, it won't be too long before I remember; especially if you are in another place Mariah, and not here on earth. I hope I wouldn't forget you for too long,' said Jo with a sad tone in his voice.

Mariah remembered that the brilliant Angel had said he would be looking after them and everyone else and that all we need do is ask. The bright Angel told them that he has lots of other little lights in his care and that he could look after all of them at the same time. 'Angels can do that,' said Mariah.

We have free will though and so they cannot interfere without our asking but they are always there nudging and whispering or leaving words. Perhaps the words could be in a book, a movie, a song, or even the wind, which makes us remember.

Jo was trying to remember some of her journey while on the planet Alcione which is in the Pleiades star system. She had said to Mariah that she wished to return there at some time to unite again for a while with some of her family there and Mariah had responded:

'Yes it is all so wonderful, we have forever to explore, and then of course to be with Father God from where we first journeyed, though I know that our Creator is always with us and in our hearts.'

Mariah also remembered a wonderful time eons ago, when she and Jo had long since left Great Mother Earth and much later they had both returned together to live on earth in a beautiful and enchanted land called Lemuria, or the Land of Mu as some people remember her.

Mariah was now with her twin flame, the beautiful little soul Jo, who had travelled with her sometimes in other galaxies or planets. She remembered that some life times they had been together and others they were in different places but still always connected in love, even if they didn't always remember this.

Chapter 2

Lemuria The Land of Mu

Life was such a joy in Lemuria which had wise souls who had come from other universes such a long distance away. Mariah and Jo could experience living in a body, to be aware of everything around them and to experience emotions while living on this beautiful blue, green and white earth planet called Gaia.

It was the third Golden Age, and Earth was shining and beautiful we could barely imagine it right now.

Mariah and Jo were full of joy and wonder at being able to experience the feelings of being in a perfect human vessel; they were as innocent joyful children.

Lemuria was a very large area of land which was where the Pacific Ocean is now, and as well as many other places surrounding, such as west coast of America nearby and Hawaii near the middle of Lemuria, though over all those aeons of time the lands and waters have changed from how they once were.

There were very wise and beautiful guardians and magnificent Angels and Archangels who looked after them and helped them to get used to their new life in this beautiful land.

The guardians taught and protected the bright little lights. The teachers and priests taught peace, love and harmony and people lived happily together then. There was no jealousy, greed or unkindness and there were no controllers. People didn't have to work hard as they enjoyed doing the things that they were happy to do and could be creative and have fun and were encouraged to use their own gifts.

The priests and elders looked to see what gifts and talents Mariah and Jo might have.

'I see Jo, you are very creative and also have the potential to be a great healer. We can see colours coming from your hands when you stroke the little animals. We will teach and show you ways as you grow so you could help others with healing; this could be with crystals, sound and colour and also aromas,' said the gentle Elder.

People didn't get ill then as everything was perfect in the beginning, but this learning would be for later on.

'Mariah, you are also creative, and you have the potential to be a wonderful teacher and story teller. You will be able to pass on the stories for the future; sometimes about your experiences in past or present times. The little children will love your stories and you will sometimes make these stories up as you go,' said the kindly priest.

And so the children were encouraged to do that which they were gifted to do and were always happy in their work and could continue to follow in this way of life. For instance if someone was gifted at artwork, painting or music, then that is the way they would be encouraged to learn rather than in later times in history where many people were unhappy in their work.

The sad 'end times' of Lemuria

Very many years later something happened to change beautiful Lemuria. There was a planet which had people on it who had gone astray and their lights were quite dim at the time and were destructive and violent and very much wanted war.

The Guardians of Light from that planet asked the guardians on earth if these wayward beings could come and live on earth so the loving people in Lemuria could be models for them and so by the loving example of the Lemurians the new residents from afar could learn to be like them and also live in harmony. After many meetings this idea was agreed to.

This worked well for hundreds of years but in the end some of the bright light souls began to copy the aggressive souls from afar, and more and more of the Lemurians had now became greedy, controlling and impatient. Their lights had now also become dim and they had forgotten where they had come from and who they really were, and were not the same loving beings any longer and were not living in harmony.

The people knew ahead that they should leave as Lemuria was going to be destroyed and some were shown the way to other areas in the Pacific including the North and South American coasts, New Zealand, Japan and Australia.

There were many loving souls that remained in connection with their Creator, however too many people had now changed for the worse and did not have love in their hearts anymore and had become greedy and dominating and sadly the age of Lemuria ended.

Some loving beings went into the other realms in the higher dimensions or to other lands, and this beautiful land of Lemuria sank down and down under the sea.

Beautiful crystal caverns of Telos

Many little bright lights went to a place called Telos which is in Mt Shasta, California. They went from Lemuria into the caves and locks which took them all the way to Telos, a magical and stunning beautiful underground world which is of a higher dimension. Some of the people went to high grounds where they had been guided.

'What happened at that time Jo? asked Mariah.

'There was a big war that destroyed the land in Lemuria. It was not pleasant living there towards the end and so some people decided to live underground. The stronger Light Beings helped the Lemurians prepare ahead of time but unfortunately many of the beautiful people on the Land of Lemuria died in the big blasts because there was not enough time to help everyone,' Jo said sadly with tears in her eyes.

'What did you do then asked Mariah?'

'I did go to Telos for a while to help the people settle in their new environment. I was one of the people that helped others to prepare to leave before it happened. Many people went through the tunnels and lived in the most beautiful underground areas at Mt Shasta and they learn very much about their spiritual side,' replied Jo.

'What was it like down there Jo?' asked Mariah.

'The surroundings were so pretty with beautiful Mother Nature, her elementals and cute little animals and inside were the most magnificent brilliant crystals, a beautiful underground world of a higher dimension of light.

The beautiful beings from Telos would like their sisters and brothers above the land to know all about them and their ways, and of course this can happen when everyone lives together once more in harmony and peace and that time will come with the new golden age approaching,' Jo replied again.

Mariah and Jo say goodbye for a while.

Mariah had left the earth plane before Jo, and before Lemuria sank. She sadly watched it all happen from above in another realm and gave her help from the dimension above.

They were separated again from the physical life, but of course were still together in spirit and remembered each other and knew that they would be together at a later time in the future.

Jo had sadly been at Mariah's side before she passed away and took her last breath on earth. Her head was held low as she was thinking how much she would miss her loving sister and all the fun they had shared together, also she remembered that they would be together again on another great adventure, but for now she knew that it was Mariah's time to go and she was ready to say goodbye to her and be happy for her new life.

Some of the people travelled a very long journey to Atlantis before Lemuria disappeared, and they lived together with the loving and gentle Atlantean people as they were in those earlier times in Atlantis. The people in Atlantis used crystal technology and later material technology and machines when they were a more mental people. The Lemurians were artistic, loving and kind and had spiritual technology which was very advanced.

'In later times the Atlanteans used the left side of their brain, they were more mental, intellectual and thought everything through all the time; whereas the Lemurians used the right side of their brain which meant they were more intuitive and creative and followed their instincts and feelings,' said Mariah.

Mariah and Jo would meet up again in Atlantis, and once more play and dance and live through another amazing lifetime together. They would again experience a different time—the Golden Age of Atlantis—the joyous times, returning again many thousands of years later towards the 'end times', to help the people with guidance and love when the Atlantian people sank lower and lower in their human ways and they once again became materialistic, greedy, controlling and in the end war, when Atlantis would be destroyed as Lemuria was destroyed.

'Remind me Jo, about Atlantis and our experiences in that past wonderful Golden Age,' Mariah asked.

'Yes, I love those memories too.'

Chapter 3

Atlantean Golden Age and 'End Times'

Once more Mariah and Jo were separated from their soul family, from their twin flames when they chose once again to return to their beautiful Gaia, Mother Earth, to experience spiritual life while being in the body, where they could experience free will and emotions in this time of the magnificent Golden Age of Atlantis.

Gaia was a planet of such beauty then as she was in the golden times of Lemuria. Her great blue seas sparkled like diamonds during the day when the sun shone on her and at night the moon lit her waters with beautiful pink and red colours. The friendly little dolphins playfully rose up and down again in the waters.

Mariah and Jo would experience life on earth again while Atlantis was in her Golden Age, when there was only harmony and perfection.

They knew that Father God and their guardians would always be there to look after them while they were on earth and that they could get guidance in those quiet moments when they listened within.

Jo and Mariah had ventured together at other times and were also together in the ancient Golden Age of Lemuria. Jo had been there in the 'end times' to help people before the land sank under the Pacific Ocean.

'Wasn't it beautiful in Lemuria?' Mariah had said to Jo.

Yes, it was so peaceful and the people so loving and friendly in those earlier times of Lemuria. They were shining and spontaneous and they lived in the moment, enjoying every moment,' replied Jo.

They both remembered that after their time in Lemuria and they had returned to the higher dimensions, their loving Guardian had invited them both to talk a little about their time down on earth while on the Land of Mu, and the two little bright lights were eager to tell their stories and experiences.

They also felt later on that they would like to return to Gaia to learn and experience even more because they wished to become even wiser and more knowing and to shine brightly and so they now wished to return to Mother Earth in this time of Golden Atlantis, to experience and learn more, all over again and do a better job this time around.

'I want to remember who I truly am', when I go back to Gaia. 'I don't want to forget the bright little light that I am, and I hope that I can help others to remember also. I want to remember about love and Father God.' said Mariah.

'Just because I will have a human form I hope it won't make me forget too much,' replied Jo.

Mariah and Jo went off together to enjoy very many more unusual and exciting experiences.

They knew that if they should forget where they had come from and that they were never alone, that they would always be connected to Father God and the beautiful light beings, and that after a time something inside them would remind them who they both were and where they had come from; those times when their minds were still and not worrying about everything they would hear the guidance. They remembered that the brilliant Angel had said the He and others would be looking after them.

And so they journeyed this time to Atlantis . . . .

Atlantis was a great and beautiful land which was where the Atlantic Ocean is now, though the land and ocean areas were different then to now on the map. Atlantis had been destroyed before and she was destroyed again over 12,000 years ago.

Some of her people managed to survive the 'end times' of the earthquakes and the giant waves that covered the land; they were able to cross a thin courseway of land from their homes in Poseida which went across to Mexico to a placed called Yucatan. Other frightened people had scrambled into boats to flee.

'Even today, thousands of years later', Jo had said, 'you can see some parts of the temples and pyramids and buildings under the sea in that area.'

'Where is that Jo?' asked Mariah.

'Many places as well as Bahamas and Florida, around the bottom of America, and the West Indies the tips of mountains came up from below the water some time after Atlantis had gone down,' Jo replied.

Jo and Mariah had remember however how beautiful and peaceful it was during the Golden Age thousands of years earlier where the people had created a paradise on this great mother earth. Everyone was very happy and enjoyed life to the full. They remembered the importance of fun and laughter and took much pleasure in using their talents and gifts as best they could.

The little bright lights had loved this wonderful golden time and enjoyed the simplicity of their lives. Much of their time was spent outdoors with Mother Nature and all her beauty and with their friends and little animal brothers who all showed unconditional love to each.

It was a time when everyone had a high frequency of light of a higher dimension and the frequency of the angels and other light beings. This was of the fifth dimension so their beautiful light was of the purest and they shone brightly with joy and happiness and they very much lived in the moment.

Mariah and Jo did not remember there ever being any disagreements among the people at that time. There was always harmony and love for each other; this included the little animals who were greatly loved and would do no harm to anyone so no one was ever afraid of them. The little animal brothers would go to school with Mariah and Jo and wait and watch patiently for them while they had their lessons outside with the elders and priests, until it was time for lunch and then would run around in excitement again. Much of their teachings were about appreciating their surrounds and the creatures and each other and they all loved unconditionally.

Teachings of the Elders

They were helped and guided with anything creative that they enjoyed and also learnt through singing, acting out a play or playing music and drawing or painting. All these creative teachings or gifts that they used would help to develop their right brain which is the side of the brain that keeps us connected to God.

'I loved my school classes' said Jo, 'remember when we were older and we were taught in the temple by the spiritual teachers and the elders. The temple was bright and there was beautiful music as well, it was all very peaceful, fun and very relaxing.'

'Yes' replied Mariah, 'I enjoyed those days also and especially when I was smaller we would learn outside amongst the beautiful trees and flowers and our little friends the fairies would come along to listen in with us sometimes. How sparkling they looked with their colourful wings of pretty lace patterns; and we knew the Angels were there, sometimes with beautiful wings of white feathers and shone brightly.'

Their left brain leaning would be to do with teachings in schools thousands of years later, for the academic subjects such as maths and science and other main subjects, whereas in the Golden Age they enjoyed creative lessons of the right brain and using their intuition.

As well as Jo being very artistic with painting, music and the arts which were all encouraged very much by the elders, she also had 'healing hands' and loved to work with crystals, music and sound.

They were taught when very young to respect others and to care about other people and their feelings and so they would not hurt each other because they realised they would be hurting themselves. They saw everything and each other as being connected.

They hadn't forgotten in those earlier days that they were connected in spirit and to God and all the beautiful bright beings and loved ones. They were taught how to see the pretty lights around the beautiful plants, animals and people and they could also see lights around plants and trees so they would know if any of nature or their friends needed help in any way; they could recognise this from the colour of the lights, which were also called the aura.

'The colours around your body were just so bright and beautiful', Mariah had said to Jo, 'sometimes they would change, but mostly they were the same and sent out wonderful feelings of calm and happiness.

Most of the people were like this,' replied Jo, 'it was such fun looking at all these shimmering colours around everything and also around the little fairies. The fairies would jump from flower to flower and slide down the branches and leaves of the trees and flowers.

'Remember Mariah, we would do that also, we would fly up to the top of the tall trees in our flying boards and fly from tree to tree. It was such a great feeling of freedom like a bird gliding up high,' continued Jo.

Mariah and Jo's home and their neighbours' homes were all circular in shape as were many homes over the ages and across the world. There was always water nearby and water flowed gently down the rocks and the sounds from this tiny waterfall made them feel relaxed while they lay in bed in the quiet of night. During the day they could dangle their feet in the cool crystal river or swim over to the boat and scramble up on it.

'Sometimes the little creatures would follow us down river and the pretty light blue and pink birds would sit on the boat watching inquisitively,' said Jo with fond memories.

The Atlantean ways

There was plenty of spare time for everyone to enjoy, relax, sit down and think wonderful thoughts and to appreciate all the precious gifts they had and their enchanting surroundings. Jo and Mariah loved to day dream and think of wonderful creations in their minds.

The people in those times only lived in the moment, they did not worry about yesterday or tomorrow, so that is why their thoughts were happy and they could appreciate everything that they focused their thoughts or eyes on at that very moment; the beauty of the flowers and the trees some called 'the tall standing ones' which made up the forest, and the clusters of bright coloured wild flowers surrounding the tree trunks.

Everyone was very loving at that time in Atlantis and everything they said or did was for the highest and greatest good of all. For instance in their thoughts, actions, their prayers or meditations they would always give thanks and be grateful for all that they had.

Their spiritual technology was quite remarkable and was always used to benefit their way of life and also for Gaia. They would not hurt or cause damage to their great mother earth who gave them their food to nourish them and her beauty. Gaia's water was always sparkling fresh and there was no pollution or rubbish put in the water then as everyone loved Mother Nature and would not harm her. The people and animals did not eat any flesh as they only ate the grains and the purest of foods that Gaia offered.

When Mariah and Jo were young as well as all the other little children, the elders would watch to see that their spiritual and psychic gifts grew as they became older and they were gently guided in the right direction. They were loving and kind and there was never any need for them to be scolded or criticised, and they had good control over their thoughts.

The elders and spiritual teachers would help them with their gifts so they could learn more about what they did best and enjoyed. They knew when they were very happy also by their aura colours shining from them. They were able to know what each others thoughts were and also could hear and see things that most people today cannot; they were also very honest.

Mariah was from a very early age interested in telling stories, she would sit and tell stories to other little children, making them up as she went along and they were magical and like fairy tales which the little ones loved. Sometimes she would have each child tell a part of the story and as they didn't know what the ending would be they would laugh when the story unfolded.

There was so much out in nature to see and talk about and get inspiration for these stories. She could see all the tiny fairies amongst nature; they would come and sit down on the grass or a pebble and listen and clap their little hands at the end of a story, also they could see the Angels with their beautiful lights and loving smiles. The elders encouraged Mariah to do more story telling as it was one of her joys.

'What did the elders say to you today Jo?' asked Mariah'.

'They told me I have healing abilities as when I stroke or hold the little animals they can tell from the colours they see emanating from my hands. They are going to help me with crystals and sound and colour; they said that all this can enhance healing. They also said that I have very good creative abilities and were encouraging me in this direction also.

I enjoyed the soft music and coloured light,' Jo continued, 'my teacher sent spiritual learning from his mind to my mind through his thoughts, Also my beautiful shining crystal I could use as a type of computer and information would come from the crystal into my forehead or my third eye it is called.'

'I had fun today at school,' said Mariah, 'we went horse riding on my pure white horse, then we went on our flying trays up quite high in the air, it was a great school trip.'

The children could fly up quite high on their little flying trays upon which they could sit quite comfortably, and of course always under the watchful eye of their parents or elders. The elders and priests could travel in the air on vehicles which were like flying coaches and they used their minds again to travel or as some would say, to teleport.

'When we were older we could draw more things to ourselves, remember Jo, all we had to do then was simply to think about a beautiful big juicy apple from the tree and we could bring it straight into our hands that way, rather than to walk over to get it,' said Mariah.

'Yes, and we could fetch our favourite toy this way too or anything else that we wished to have; also the elders could attract energy from a long way up and bring it down for the people to use and also very beneficial for Gaia,' responded Jo.

'We didn't really need to speak in words as we could speak with our minds by our thoughts and the other person could easily understand, though it was exciting to have the choice to also be able to speak with our voices if we chose,' continued Jo.

'Would you like that orange from that tree over there?' Mariah had said to Jo who replied yes that she would have that big bright one at the top, and so Jo brought it to her by his thoughts.

This was not unusual for those times as everyone could do it. They could focus on something and it would appear as if magically from the thin air, though they did also enjoy using their hands and to walk to fetch something. Jo and Mariah also enjoyed using their hands to make something creative from the soil mixed with water. They were very artistic and loved to paint and usually got their colours from the dyes of the plants.

They were always thankful and appreciated all that they could use and were always loving towards God's creatures from the animal kingdom as well as the plant kingdom.

They were so close to nature in those times, their senses were very fine tuned and they could see and hear things that most of us could not today. They enjoyed the simplicity of dangling their feet in the stream in the crystal clear water and looking at their faces as if looking in a mirror; they loved to pull funny faces to make each other laugh and their little magical friends would be there laughing with them.

'Look Jo, here come our fairy friends to play, the little sisters to the angels in their dazzling tunics of many colours and their lacy wings. We can play 'hide and seek' in the woods together.' They all laughed and played and their lives were filled with fun and joy.

The faeries were always in the garden waiting for them to play. Sometimes they would hide and Jo and Mariah had to search for them; they could also blend in with the trees if they wished or make themselves disappear and appear again in another place, they all laughed and laughed.

All the glowing people in the time of Golden Atlantis were so very appreciative that they were able to have come to live on great Mother Earth for this experiment which was to see if they could keep their Divine connection to God and all the beautiful light beings as well as live in a body at the same time.

They felt very grateful that they could experience what it was like to touch the beautiful trees and flowers, to taste the food, to smell the beautiful perfume of the flowers and also to see these wondrous creations of nature. It was so exciting to experience these physical senses while in their human vessel and to be there at such an innocent time.

Everything in nature was in harmony and the people and the animals were happy together. The gardens were as pretty as a beautiful picture and the fruit trees abundant in colour and fruit. Because they were at one with everything they would never pick a flower without first asking the flower and they would not kill any animal because they saw everything as equal and in a loving way. They saw the sweet little animals as harmless and as their brothers and sisters.

Mothers and fathers always showed love and kindness to each other and were a wonderful example to their children who learnt from this and this example was a fine way to be taught. They were able to get close to the little soul of their baby even before the little one had been born into this world.

They would sing and talk and this would give happy vibrations to the little one. As they grew older the little ones always felt loved and very special. They learnt from the examples of their parents as well as their elders and teachers who were always kind, loving and gave much encouragement to the children.

The elder spiritual teachers could see from the colours of the lights around the children as to what spiritual gifts they had and this would be looked after and very much encouraged as they grew older. Because of this they would not be unhappy during their lives doing jobs that they didn't enjoy or were not gifted to do.

Rather they did the things that they were best suited to do and used the spiritual gifts that they were born with and so were contented and enjoyed everything they did. They also enjoyed a lot of time having fun and relaxing; they played and sang and danced around laughing with joy.

Sometimes in the garden a beautiful white unicorn would come and stand beside Mariah and Jo, her name was Snowy; her light shone very brightly from her forehead in the shape of a horn. Snowy was a wonderful reminder to them that they were very precious and as pure as their little bright lights which came from the Divine heart of our Creator.

'I am going to ask Snowy to give me a special wish,' Mariah had said to Jo. She often saw her while playing in the forest, sometimes it would be pure white and other times it would be slightly invisible like a beautiful soft cloud.

Often Snowy would invite the children to ride on her back and they would go slowly around the trees alongside the stream down to the lake where the boats were and sit on the water edge and watch parents with their children laughing and playing in the sparkling water. Snowy had beautiful bright eyes which looked lovingly at the Jo and Mariah and made them feel so special.

Temples of crystal

'Remember the elder who was in charge of our area. He was such a beautiful person as were the elders from other places,' said Mariah.

'He was a very advanced and spiritual soul with special powers. The elders could contact other beings in other worlds or planets up in the sky, and tell us stories about our brothers and sisters from the other planets and where some of us had also come from during one of our experiences. I was told that I had once come from a star called Alcione,' said Jo.

This special time was a cosmic experiment on Gaia and it was to see if the little bright lights could live in a human body and experience emotions. To know what it feels like to taste the berries and the fruits that they were grateful to eat, to smell the beauty of the flowers and hear the beautiful pure sounds of the crystal and the birds and animal brothers talking to them in their own way. And as well as experiencing all this, to see if they could still at the same time keep close to God and not forget who they were, the Divine little souls or little bright lights from their Creator's heart centre.

For many hundreds of years all went well . . . .

'Remember Jo, in that wonderful Golden Age when we were young students being taught lessons on healing and we were in those magnificent pyramid buildings made of brilliant shining crystal or marble; we learnt a lot there and in some of the pyramids the elders could bring down the energies so the people could use the power for their works and homes,' said Mariah.

'Yes, I remember, there were different temples, in one for instance you could learn about healing, or in another to learn all about the beauty and benefits of sound. Also there was a temple where people could be made to feel fresh and energetic again, and wonderful learning was taught there.' replied Jo.

'I can remember the exquisite crystalline light shining brightly over the temples all the time and light in different colours was luminous and unlike colours we could imagine today and crystals of absolute beauty for different uses, and in another area there was an amazing Great Crystal,' continued Jo.

'We had our very own special little crystals and the power from the big crystal would come through the lines of a system into our little ones, then we could ask any question that we wished to know the answer to, and the answer would come into our third eye area in the middle of our forehead.

.I remember the Magi dressed in his gown of brilliant red violet; a very wise and spiritual man of importance, and he would put information into my tiny crystal when I was in the temple and I could take it away and learn from this.

There were also bigger crystals and the priests would use these for healing and also for teaching. Every intention was asked for the greatest and highest good as they knew to ask for this would be for the best outcome because people don't always know the bigger picture or how things will work out,' said Mariah.

'We were always happy and healthy in the early days of Atlantis and so didn't really need much healing, though I remember our parents loved to go along to the temple to see the priest for therapy with crystals and sound and we would like to sit nearby and watch the priest. In the beginning we really only needed our energy kept healthy and well and we knew how to do that then, by our happy thoughts and way we lived our lives in balance and harmony.' said Jo.

'Later on as the years passed sound, colour and sometimes herbs and beautiful fragrant aromas from the garden were used, and people could talk to the healer priest if they had anything they were worried about and he could help people sort things out.

They were very skilled and they would sometimes use a crystal laser rod for psychic surgery to take away anything that was not healthy,' said Mariah.

'I was very interested in watching and listening at healings, as that was what I wanted to do as I became older,' said Jo.

'Yes, I feel that we could all do well in these present times to remember to use some of those methods of healing, in fact there are many people that do use them already and more are beginning to do so as people are wanting to be more relaxed and balanced. They are realising they need fun and laughter and relaxation in their lives,' replied Mariah.

'If people had any unhappy thoughts or feelings back then they could call and see, what was called 'The Violet Flame' and this would help them feel good again; the flame was not hot of course, it was a beautiful bright light and when it was time for people to leave the great mother earth they would go into the Violet Flame which was in a temple, and when they walked into this flame they would go straight to a different place in another dimension and world,' said Mariah; 'they would go back to where they came from on their journey back to God.'

'I notice that you said 'leave' Mariah, and not 'die' as no one ever dies when it is their time to leave Gaia, they don't die, they just change their form. That is the way it was meant to be in the beginning Mariah, people were not meant to be ill and suffer when it is their time to leave.' Jo responded.

'I know, not the way it would be in later lives when the times were not golden any more and where people would sometimes suffer before they died, that is so sad,' Mariah had said. 'A lot of illness is caused by fear, people worry themselves sick sometimes, they have forgotten how to have fun and do the things that they enjoy so much and to relax and live in harmony with each other and nature,' Mariah continued.

'Yes, they will have forgotten how to live in the moment because if they did this they would not worry about yesterday or worry about tomorrow. They would be able to enjoy that very moment, to see and appreciate the beautiful flowers or the ripples in the river, without the mind being all over the place and busy with too many thoughts,' added Jo.

Jo and Mariah were now playing with their little dolphin brothers. They knew the dolphins understood cosmic knowledge and looked after it in their brain as if it was a computer.

'I do sometimes love to use my mind to speak to Dolly,' said Mariah. 'It feels different to speak, but sometimes it is fun to use my thoughts for a change when I speak and learn from the dolphins, and I know she gives me guidance and joy.'

Dolly was Mariah's dolphin and Little Jo was Jo's dolphin.

'It is such fun swimming with them, they are like brilliant Guardian Angels and so wise,' said Jo. 'I know that they will always help us all even far into the future when times are darker, they will remind us then how it was when we were in the Golden Age and Gaia was beautiful like heaven on earth. We will be reminded that these beautiful times will come back again because the magnificent Golden Age has come and gone, more than once, and it is coming again.

Jo and Mariah had now long left Golden Atlantis, they left before many people had turned to greed and anger and had become dishonest with each other and had just forgotten how to love.

Jo had gone back to a beautiful planet where she once lived called Alcione, the Great Central Sun of the Pleiades group up in the stars, the sky which looks so beautiful when looking up from Gaia at night.

After Mariah had taken her last breath on earth, her eternal little bright light went back into another dimension in the spirit world from where she had came.

She loved being with her loved ones again, the lovely serene surrounds and the beauty, even more beautiful than Atlantis. She knew that though Mariah and she were in different places they were still together and would meet up again soon and have more wonderful adventures, for they had travelled the universe together before.

The Law of One and the Atla-Ra from the Island of Poseida

Many thousands of years later Mariah and Jo knew Atlantis had changed and the Golden Age had become less golden, and Atlantis had split into different islands. There were two main big islands now and they were ruled by two very different groups of people; it was still beautiful at this stage but unfortunately it could not remain that way.

One group had stayed innocent and true to their Creator and they were called The LAW OF ONE and lived in the beautiful Emerald City on the Island of Poseida and this was the main area for the crystalline power. This Island was magnificent and there were also tunnels which could go to different dimensions in the heavens.

Crystalline light shone brightly over the temples all the time in different colours which were luminous and unlike anything we could imagine today. The crystals there were absolutely beautiful and used in different ways. Mariah and Jo were often in wonder at the beauty of all the magnificent lights and they never forgot this.

They had both learnt about healing in the Golden Age in a great pyramid. Some of these pyramids were made of marble or crystal. In one pyramid elders would bring down the energies to the grid for power so that the people could use this power in their works and in their homes and also for Gaia's beautiful lands.

Poseida had beautiful temples which were all different and the people could go to them for either healing, learning, or if they wanted to feel energised again and the learning taught there was wonderful.

The elders and spiritual teachers would help them with their gifts so they could learn more about what they did best and enjoyed, so they were very happy learning as were encouraged to follow the path of their gifts, whether it be healing, teaching, art or any other type of creativity or work that they enjoyed and because they were happy in their studies they did very well.

'I remember at that time Jo, there were some very tall people who were considered to be the 'Golden Race' of Atlantis,' said Mariah. 'In the beginning these 'tall ones' came from the Pleiadean planet far away in the sky. They were about 11 feet tall and big and kind like gentle giants. I did love being with them and learning and hearing their stories of their other planet. They worked with the people and taught them. They were very artistic and creative and their teaching was fun.

The Law of One people had very beautiful hearts and they believed that everything was one and connected, and so if you hurt someone else you hurt yourself. They hadn't forgotten who they were and where they had come from,' Mariah continued.

'Then there were the ATLA-RA priests who were very scientific as well and had also remained connected to Father God. They too lived in Poseida, they were very clever and wise and they looked after the crystal power grids. They could read other people's minds and were in touch with other planets way up in the beautiful star sprinkled sky, including two planets called Sirius and Pleiades.

It was so wonderful looking up at the stars at night Mariah, I have a memory of us sitting there on the hill. You were in a mauve tunic with your long fair hair and I was also in mauve. We were in awe of the beauty up there as we watched the stars and the patterns some of them made and some would shoot down very quickly in the glittering sky,' said Jo.

'The priests there in those times lived very, very long lives as they could use their minds in a positive and happy way and also they could go into the Rejuvenation Temple if they wished to have more energy and to be made to feel good again. Some even lived for thousands of years and so this is how their amazing crystal and spiritual technology had been kept for such a long time.

It was so much more advanced than anything people of future ages would have. The crystals gleamed and shone and some had many facets,' continued Jo.

'So our brothers and sisters who had stayed close to their Creator and remembered who they were and where they had come from, were called the Law of One, the Golden Race, and the Atla-Ra priests who lived in Poseida,' said Mariah.

The Sons of Belial from the Island of Aryan

'Yes, and the other group were called the SONS OF BELIAL and they lived on an Island which was called Aryan, but after a while the Aryans became controlling and greedy and very materialistic, and so instead of living in love they lived in fear of losing their wealth and their power,' said Jo.

'Very much the same story as that which happened at the 'end times' of Lemuria, as although then many loving souls remained in connection with their Creator, too many people had changed for the worse and did not have love in their hearts anymore and they had become controlling and very greedy, very similar to what happened in the 'end times' of Atlantis.

'At that time in Atlantis, thousands of years ago, white people ruled Aryan and they thought they were better than everyone else. They controlled the money and were in charge of everything and everyone, even though most of the other people had red bronze skin.

The Aryans became dishonest and more powerful and wanted to cause problems for the Law of One in any way that they possibly could. They wanted the crystalline power technology for war and to control the world and to use people as slaves and soldiers,' said Mariah.

'So for several thousands of years nothing happened between the two groups. The Poseidans were gentle and loving and believed that they would get the Aryans to change by the loving words and example of the Poseidans, but not so!

Aryans were only interested in power and control and were cunning and untrustworthy, but they were very worried that if they didn't watch their ways the Poseidans would close off the crystalline energy and of course they needed this for their machines and for their every day living,' continued Mariah.

'When war came Aryans wanted the crystalline power but Poseida would definitely not agree to this as they were aware of the real dangers if this power was in their hands, and so unfortunately they had to shut down the power which now meant that the Aryans had no supply for food or goods and could not work without it.

So big problems! and the cunning and sly Aryans came up with the idea that both sides should have someone in charge of talks so as to bring back peace and harmony as it had been earlier in the Golden times. They really could not be trusted though,' said Jo.

'Sons of Belial happened to have a well-liked leader. He had an appealing and clever way with words and was able to trick all into thinking everything would once more become as it was in the beautiful Golden Age, but really all they wanted was to use the crystal beam for war. Sadly their lies and their false promises were believed by the kindly Poseidans who had been tricked very badly,' continued Mariah.

As a result the Aryans now unfortunately held the crystal power and had become even more controlling than before.'

The magnificent Crystal Second Moon Satellite

'Do you remember the magnificent crystalline satellite, Mariah? it was called the Second Moon of Atlantis. It was massive, and the Arcturians had come from their home planet very far away in the heavens, they had come to build this great satellite?' asked Jo.

'Yes, I do remember. In the evenings when we were sitting on the hill looking up into the magnificent deep blue sky we would see not one, but two beautiful moons. In the distance we could see the silver moon amongst millions of diamond stars and closer to us was the Second Moon of Atlantis, the sparkling satellite of crystal. That was real beauty!' exclaimed Mariah.

'There was a kindly scientist working this beautiful gleaming crystal satellite and sadly he knew that the end was about to come for the 'Crystal Moon', because the healing crystals, some of which were very many facetted and sparkled like diamonds in the light, as well as the fire crystals and the power grids which were crystalline, were now run by the controllers the ones that could not be trusted and that was so sad Jo.'

'These beautiful crystals were controlled by this great satellite. When the beams were sent to the great satellite they would be cleansed and made better. These rays also helped farmers with their little creatures and amongst other things these beams were used for the healing temples.'

'That certainly was a grand satellite, a bright enormous sparkling moon in the sky with rainbow colours spinning and glowing lights spreading out into the sky in all directions, so lovely to look at,' remembered Jo.

'Unfortunately then a scientist from the wrong side sent damaging beams to start earthquakes against countries that did not do as they said. There was a lot of ruin caused near Europe because of these harmful beams, then the beautiful 'Crystal Moon' had lost its strength and now nothing could be done to make it right again.

Our brothers from the planet Sirius B came to the aid beforehand, though alas Crystal Moon crashed down to Mother Earth causing the most awful explosions.

The ones that had stayed close to their Creator, the Atla–Ra and Law of One, now had to break the connection of the crystals from the beautiful big Crystal Moon and then they took the crystals to a place where they could not be found. Crystal Moon had acted as a 'brain', similar to that of a computer, but the reason they had to break the connection was to protect the other crystals,' said Mariah.

'I understand Jo, that some crystals were put in a tunnel under the ground and this was done with help again from our friends from Sirius B,' said Mariah.

'Yes, and also some crystals were sent to areas such as Brazil, and put in places that could not be seen by human eyes because these locks were of another dimension; then the crystals were made unworkable,' said Jo.

'That would be similar to Lemuria at the 'end times' before she sank, some people had gone into tunnels and locks and into a higher dimension there and it is said that in later times they had been seen out walking amongst the beauty of nature in a place called Mt Shasta in California. They were seen to be wearing white tunics,' interrupted Mariah, changing the subject.

The 'end times' of Atlantis

'Yes I remember that experience Mariah, and I was one of the people that helped others to escape at the 'end times' of Lemuria.

However returning to our remembering of Atlantis and the 'end times', the great crystal satellite crashed and made the shield at the bottom of the Atlantic Ocean very weak, leaving millions of pieces of crystals far down under the deep blue Atlantic Ocean. You could see great smoke clouds in the sky like a curtain hiding the sun so everything became dark and not very pleasant looking.

There were earthquakes and the water came up like giant gushing waves covering the land and taking everything in their path and the crystal power stations blew up in pieces creating bright red and yellow flames of light like massive sparklers in the dark; it was horrific,' said Jo.

'So really it was the earthquakes that destroyed these remaining islands of Atlantis!' Mariah asked.

'Yes, the earthquakes started the massive tidal waves, and also as well as the destruction of Atlantis, crystal pieces left after a big explosion of a power station can be seen near Brazil and also destroyed were some parts of the west side of Africa. Remember Mariah that Atlantis was an enormous area of land and the areas of water and land would be different to how they are on the map today,' replied Jo.

'A couple of weeks after those big tidal waves, all the land went under the sea but fortunately before Atlantis sank some of the people were able to cross a thin stretch of land which was not yet covered with water. This strip of land went from their homes in Poseida all the way across the water to Mexico to a place called Yucatan.

It makes you realise Mariah just how big Atlantis was if they could travel this distance from one to the other. You could also see very frightened and hungry people scrambling into any boat that they could manage to climb aboard. They were very weak at this stage but determined to do the best that they could to try to get to safety though there was not much time for them to do this before the land went completely under the sea.

'Even today, thousands of years later,' Jo continued, 'I understand that you can see some parts of the temple, pyramids and building ruins under the sea in that area.'

'Where is that Jo?'

'Many places, but also the Bahamas and Florida, around there, which is down the bottom of America and the West Indies; the tips of mountains came up from below the water some time after Atlantis had gone down.

There are remnants reportedly scattered, amongst them the Bumini Islands thought to be part of an Atlantean mountain range and ruins of roads and buildings near the island and also under the waters near Morocco.

Documentation mentions remains of roads, pyramids and relics found at the bottom of the waters stretching from the Bahamas and over to the African and European coastal areas. As well as America there was some remains found in the Yucatan, also the Pyrenees, etc., of a dynasty no longer in existence,' Jo replied.

However, long, long before the sinking of Atlantis, Mariah and Jo had experienced a wonderful lifetime in the Golden Age of Atlantis.

Winds of Change

Mariah and Jo had a special love for great Mother Earth with all her beauty and her loving little creatures and this would be why they would both return to be with Mother Earth Gaia and their brothers and sisters at this special time we are now living in.

They and many other souls wished to be here to experience ascension into another dimension of beauty and harmony, with the Atlantean energy once again here, and the coming into another perfect and magnificent Golden Age. The beautiful and perfect Golden Age has come and gone more than once, and it is coming again when all will be in harmony.

'So as you were saying Mariah, it will be like the golden ages of Lemuria and Atlantis, when it was like heaven on earth and the people loved their lives and used their gifts and so were very contented. They danced and laughed and loved their loyal animal companions and enjoyed the beauty of nature with all her wonders. They were in harmony with everything,' said Jo.

'We can focus on beauty, goodness and love, as you said Mariah. This darkness has got well out of balance. We could visualise beautiful pictures in our minds of everyone and everything and each one of us living in harmony and to feel that we are one with our Father God and all of God's creation. We could begin to remember the beauty of those Golden Times of Lemuria and Atlantis when it was like heaven on earth,' Jo continued.

'Yes Jo, we have journeyed through time and space to come here to have our experiences and to learn from them and then we move back through time again on our way back to Father God. That is certainly some journey!' replied Mariah as they sat there on the grass surrounded by the beautiful elementals and sweet little animals.

Chapter 4

The Angelics

The beautiful Angels are coming closer to us these days more than ever before and they bring to us their unconditional love, guidance and their brilliance. They want to let us know and understand their world and where they come from. To remind us about our magnificence and to help us remember the beautiful beings that we truly are and where we have come from. We would not be able to comprehend at present the beautiful places we have come from and where we have been.

We could not possibly comprehend this while in our limited human vessel.

During these times of great change, the winds of change that we are now experiencing, the beautiful Angelics are helping with this transition. Mankind is coming of age and our consciousness is expanding further afield as we are now starting to explore our solar system and even beyond there.

If we choose we can receive their wonderful gifts and accept that these beautiful Angelic beings are here with us. We can also call upon any of the great Light Beings, the Archangels and the Ascended Masters. We can ask them to over-light us and call on any of these light beings whichever feels right for us, and of course Father God our Creator is always there in our hearts and with us.

. . . . *The story begins long ago* when Mariah and Jo were sitting at their computer screen and just 'out of the blue' the screen changed and there suddenly appeared a new page in front of their eyes. Their eyes grew even wider with amazement because this page was nothing to do with anything they were looking for.

This new page was all about Archangels and Angels and had not been on their minds at the time. They had learnt about angels when they were very young, however this came to them again suddenly and unexpectedly.

Mariah and Jo looked surprised and realized that this was an unusual thing to happen but yet they both wanted to keep learning more about the angels. They could not stop looking at the screen, they were quite mesmerised and spent the whole day on the computer reading about these beautiful Archangels and Angels. The time passed so quickly it only seemed a short while and each time they clicked on to a new subject there appeared so many more stories and information about these magnificent Beings.

Ever since that day they have both loved knowing that their angels were around and have learnt so much about them and also had some exciting and unusual experiences with their angels.

Going back in time though, many eons ago, two little bright lights came from the heart centre of our Creator's heart and on down from the Great Central Sun and the seven spheres. There were many other little bright lights which you could also call little souls and they were all very special.

Many have the essence of angels in their heart soul and are of angelic lineage and each little bright light is as important as the next, just a different facet of our Creator God.

The little bright lights ventured to different beautiful galaxies and planets and many other worlds in the universe and to a very special planet further away called earth, 'Lady Gaia' in beautiful colours of exquisite green, blue and white. The little animals on Mother Earth were so cute, loving and playful as were the beautiful glowing beings at that time.

Mother Earth was just a little planet and different to the other planets as on this planet the people would have the physical form of a body to cover their bright little light. These beautiful little Divine sparks would have physical form and would help build a paradise on earth.

Mariah and Jo had had many wonderful experiences at different times in Gaia's history and had seen the wonderful golden ages of Lemuria and Atlantis as well as the 'end times' thousands of years later.

Jo and Mariah were now here experiencing and living on the beautiful Gaia, the Great Mother Earth. Since their experience on the computer when the Archangel Website appeared unexpectedly and even before that, they had loved the Angels and Archangels very much and had some wonderful experiences. They knew that these beautiful bright beings were their guardians and would help them along the way whenever they needed and asked for help, and that they would get a gentle nudge sometimes to guide them in the right direction. Yes, they had many experiences with their loving and gentle Angels, and some quite unusual experiences.

Mariah remembered being driven on very icy dangerous roads, more dangerous than the driver realised at the time.

She suddenly noticed a car driving very slowly in front of them for a very long distance. The road was extremely quiet with not a car in sight and yet here appeared this car for such a long time, driving very slowly in front of them making it impossible for them to overtake because of the narrow and steep windy roads.

Mariah felt very strongly that this was an Angel there to protect them from the icy conditions.

'Do you remember that Jo, we were together sitting in the back seat? The roads were very winding and we were at times very high up in the mountains looking down. We didn't hear until later that people were advised not to travel or at least should have wheel chains though we had been unable to purchase any wheel chains,' asked Mariah.

'Yes, that was quite strange for the car from nowhere to slow us down,' replied Jo. 'Perhaps it was our Guardian Angel or Archangel Michael.

I also remember having lots of nudges which were like strong thoughts or feelings of warnings not to do something and I knew later that this had been for my safety or other times for my help.

One day I clearly saw some beautiful bright lights in my bedroom and knew they were Angels, and I have seen beautiful orbs of bright white light. I also know when my angels are there or confirming something I am saying, because I will see coloured lights and patterns in front of my eyes like a kaleidoscope that you look through. I know always this is a sign for me that the angels are right there with me,' continued Jo.

'When I was a tiny toddler and walking down the street with my beautiful mother holding on to my hand, I somehow pulled away from her. I was told that I ran straight out into the busy road in a flash and that there was a car coming towards me. Mother screamed out and in an instant the car stopped just a few inches from my little frame. That was a miracle I had been told and I think also that there was Divine intervention and was not my time to go,' said Mariah.

'I always go very shivery or tingly in my legs when I need to hear certain things and that is confirmation for me. I know it is the Angels letting me know the answer is correct,' said Jo.

'That is exactly what happens to me, I go shivery and tingling all over and it is such a strong feeling each time to let me know,' replied Mariah.

'Also, if you see a feather where there are not lots of birds around then this can be a sign that an Angel is there, or it could mean an answer to something you may be thinking of at that exact time. Some people call a white feather an 'Angel's calling card'.

'Jo, remember the extraordinary thing that happened when mother was very ill in hospital and she was unconscious. We put a music CD of gentle Angelic music into the CD player but instead it played completely different music which was piano music instead of the angelic music. It so happened that our mother loved piano music and would play it every night before she went to sleep.

We had wondered had we put on the wrong CD. It was lovely listening to the piano music and I am sure that even though mother was unconscious she would have heard her favourite music. Do you think that the Angels were playing this music for her?' asked Mariah.

'Yes, I think so, because when we arrived home we checked to see if it was in fact the piano music we had played by mistake, but no, the original angelic music was now back on the CD, meaning that the music had mysteriously changed to piano,' said Jo.

Voice of the Wind Mariah

'Also Joe, remember how the writing of these books come about. I was lying in bed listening to the wind which was very strong and the thought came to my mind—'**They call the Wind Mariah**' and the Winds of Change, and that is how it all started. So this must have been the Angels or a beautiful Being of Light, and look how quickly the writing of the books came about.

Within a short time I had written 7 children's books and another large book. Sure I had accumulated or remembered that which I had gained over many years from great teachers, from intuition and from a great imagination. I still had to add to, and make some changes but the storyline and putting together of all these books was done in that short period, and it came fast, passionate and inspirational,' said Mariah.

'I think that is quite amazing, so lots of help there I think Mariah and they are written in a different way and it is the right time for this information to be out there to remind us of our magnificent heritage and so that we can visualize a new Golden Age,' replied Jo.

'Jo, then there was another extraordinary incident, the time you were woken up at 4 a.m. in the morning and went straight down to the computer. You looked on a website and instantly up came a house advertisement which sounded perfect.

You then waited impatiently for the estate agent to open premises to answer the phone and ask for a viewing. That was the house you bought and it is so beautiful and up on a hill as you had wished for. Lovely and serene and surrounded by Mother Nature and all the beautiful trees; the house of your dreams! You were obviously guided to find this house as it came about in such a strange way and after about a year of looking unsuccessfully for houses,' said Mariah.

'Yes, we were at the end of our tether, we had been let down quite a few times before but knew instantly that this home shown on the computer at 4.00 a.m. was going to be the one for us. We must have been guided because it was perfect for us, everything went smoothly.

The owners had just put a new roof on the house and it was everything we wanted, even the grounds had been landscaped ready for us to put our finishing touches and designs to. I feel that this would have been 'Divine Timing, the right time for us,' said Jo.

Angels are also known by many different religions such as the Jewish, Christian and Islamic, and also other people who aren't religious at all but still could be kind and loving people and believe in God. They just know that these beautiful beings of light are nearby and patiently waiting to be asked for their help and so many people do put their trust in their Angels.

'The Angels won't step in unless we ask because they know that we have free will,' said Mariah. 'So we just need to ask and they nearly always give the help that we need. If not then I think that it is not meant to be just at that precise time,' Mariah continued. 'Perhaps it is to do with 'Divine Timing' again, which we don't understand the full picture of such things.'

'These beautiful beings are pure spiritual beings from the heart of Father God. They do not judge us at all and they see the love in each and every one of us through eyes of love. We also have a Guardian Angel who is with us for a lifetime and in other lifetimes as well.

At times we may hear them speak perhaps through a song, or it could be through another person in the words they speak. Those words may mean something special to us at that time or might give us an idea to do something different. Maybe on the radio we might hear a few words that will let us know what we wanted to know which will help us.

It could also be words in a book to make us think about an idea, or nudge us or jolt our memory to remind us we have something to do,' added Jo.

'Angels are full to the brim of unconditional love so they are a wonderful example to us. Whatever we do they will still love us and they are always there to help us when we ask though they cannot step in if it is our time to leave this earth. For instance if a person were in a fatal car accident then the Angels cannot stop that from happening if it is time for that person to die,' said Mariah.

'The Angels would be there to help in other ways though Mariah I am sure, and comforting those loved ones nearby,' responded Jo.

'However if someone is about to have an accident and it is not yet their time to depart this life, then the Angels can come and help without our permission. That is the only time they can do this, if it is not our time to die.'

We never die, we just change form

We never die though Jo, when our time has come to pass over, we just change form. Instead of our human body we will change and have a different form but otherwise we are still the same little bright light and we carry on in our new life learning and experiencing.

So we shouldn't be too sad for too long if we lose a loved one as it is their time to go and they will have done all that they chose to do on earth before they were born. They will be meeting up with loved ones that were sad to see them leave when they first came down to be born in the human body here on Gaia. They will be with us in spirit along the way, enjoying the things we love to do and comforting us when we are sad and then the day we ourselves pass over they will all be there to lovingly greet us,' said Mariah.

'That is a nice thought to know that we are never parted from our loved ones for long and we will meet up with them again and again. So either we will be welcoming them with open arms or they will be welcoming us lovingly,' said Jo.

'We are never really parted anyway, either from our loved ones or the Angels. We have just forgotten who we really are and where we have come from as after we were born we forget most of this; a veil comes across our memory.

Sometimes little children will see their loved ones or the Angels or Fairies, and play with them out in the garden. They are invisible to mum and dad who will wonder who the children are talking to and playing with. They think that they are imaginary friends they are playing with,' said Maria.

'Though sometimes it is not the little children's imagination, they really are playing and seeing other bright little lights that are not in the body as we are. They are having fun and playing out in the garden amongst the woods and wild flowers; they are having tea parties and dancing and laughing and playing as children do,' added Joe.

'Some children and sometimes even adults can see Angels and other light beings but mainly children can and as they get older and become more used to other people and the world around them, these beautiful beings are still nearby but can't be seen any longer; they are there still whispering guidance or helping when asked, said Mariah.

'We can ask our Angelics for anything at all as long as it is honest and right and it will help if we make our request clear. We should not ask in a selfish way and the request or prayer should be for the best intentions and we should remember to thank the Angels because they will very much appreciate our kindness. Also it is best if we do not complain when asking or praying because if our thoughts are unhappy and worried then this puts a little cloud around us and it is more difficult for the Angels to get close to us,' said Jo.

'When we think about God and the Angels or nature and the lovely little animals and creatures and think happy thoughts, the Angels are attracted to us as our thoughts can put a path between the Angels and us and they can come closer.

We can sometimes then great ideas or thoughts. At times strange things happen that make us know that our Angels are with us and helping; we will know this because the feeling will be loving and peaceful. As I said earlier I also get a tingling or shivery feeling run through me and I know it is the Angels. It happens when I am saying or thinking about something and would like it to be confirmed,' said Mariah.

The Angels like fun also and usually aren't too serious and so they are very happy and excited when they see us laughing or dancing, anything that makes us feel wonderful. They want to join in and experience our happiness and joy.

'I like to a talk or pray to my Angels and God,' said Mariah. 'Though it doesn't matter at all if some people prefer to ask either their Angels, Father God, Jesus or other Masters or Light Beings, because God is not forgotten as they are an extension of Father God, they are all as one and they will all help us and guide us.'

'Yes, Mariah, we could see the Angels as helpers, as part of God. They are all loving beings and who love us unconditionally and want to help us every time we ask.

As well as the Angels and Guardian Angels, there are also the great Archangels who are magnificent beings of light. The Angels are under the direction of Archangels and there are many though here are a few of the most well known Archangels,' said Mariah.

Mighty Archangels

Archangel Michael

Colour Sapphire blue. He is an excellent Archangel to ask for help if we want protection and will keep us safe and give us strength and courage; he also helps policemen and leaders. He is the guardian overlord of the Angels, the elementals and each one of us and he will make sure that every one of us comes back to the perfect beings that we are.

He can cut away any fears with his large sword and release them. Archangel Michael is known as the greatest of all the

Angels in writings around the world and this includes the Christian, Islamic and Jewish religions.

Archangel Michael has said that the Archangels are all that we here on earth are, but that they are also much more as well; that they are all the time in tune with our Creator and that the Will of the Archangels is in perfect harmony with Father God's will,' said Mariah.

'I feel that I particularly resonate with Archangel Michael as I always feel drawn to asking him for help and I know that he will protect me with his beautiful blue cloak of protection any time that I ask and this makes me feel loved and secure. I also like to ask him sometimes to clear a space, perhaps a room from another's negativity.

I know that he is looking after each and every one of us and protecting us. I like to ask Archangel Michael to protect me or my home with his beautiful blue cloak of protection.

'I don't forget my Guardian Angel though who as all the Angels loves us unconditionally, helps us with our inspiration and also protects and guides us along our way,' said Jo.

Archangel Gabriel

All the Archangels have wonderful jobs that they do, for instance Archangel Gabriel works with the white ray of purity, colour of shining white. He came to tell Mary the news about Baby Jesus and helps us with communication. He helps spiritual leaders, musical people and writers and he also brings joy and clarity.

He will help us to be sympathetic, to understand others, help us to be more generous and make our negative emotions purified. He helps spiritual leaders and scientists, astronomers and musicians and much more. So we can ask for help with any of those qualities.

Archangel Jophiel

Works with the golden yellow ray, and helps with the arts; he inspires and lights up our minds and helps us to become wise. He will help with learning and so therefore is very helpful for students, teachers and artistic people. We can ask for help with these qualities, and to help us be joyful, and as with all the Angels we should remember to say 'THANK YOU'.

Archangel Chamuel

Works with the pink ray of love, and she helps artists and people that like to make peace and helps with our relationships. She helps us find love and compassion and to forgive others; perhaps someone may have hurt us.

She will help the flame of love in your heart to become bigger and brighter, so we could ask Archangel Chamuel to help with compassion and forgiveness, perhaps unforgiveness is holding us back and we can ask for help with this.

Archangel Raphael

Works with the emerald green ray of healing and of plenty, so she helps with healing and she has a band of healing Angels. She helps travellers and also ensures we have ample.

She is nearby and helps surgeons, doctors and also electricians etc. So we could ask Archangel Raphael to help us if we are travelling, for healing for ourselves or others and we can also ask or for abundance.

Archangel Uriel

The gold and purple ray of peace and wisdom. He is very helpful if there are conflicts or arguments. He helps missionaries and people working on the land, and he will send the angels of peace to make us feel calmer; he helps us to be peaceful and to shine light on our path.

He also helps free us from our fears, so if we are fearful or afraid we could ask Archangel Uriel. We can always ask any of the Angels or Archangels, as if we are not sure who to ask for what, then we could just ask for the appropriate angel for the task for we wish to have help or to help others.

Archangel Zadkiel

The violet ray of transmutation for cleansing. He helps people to be more forgiving and patient. He also works with St Germaine and the Violet Flame. The Angels of Mercy, Transmutation and Joy are under his command. You could ask Archangel Zadkiel to free you from negativity, to be more forgiving of others and to be more patient.

Archangel Metatron

Archangel Metatron whose colour is brilliant white, has a particular place for children in his heart and he loves to assist spiritually talented children such as the Indigo and the Crystal Children. Archangel Metatron helps us with our enlightenment and to spiritually evolve.

'These special children are new children coming through now aren't they Mariah? I understand that there have been and are new children coming through and when they grow up they will be in leadership jobs and will bring about fairness and help with the new world.

When they were born they already had a lot of wisdom they would remember and not have to spend a whole life time like we did having to learn. They will already know much more and be very wise for their years, or I should say they have not forgotten it all like we did with the veil of forgetfulness when we came to earth.

The Crystal children are under the supervision of Archangel Metatron. He leads the children both in heaven and on Gaia, Great Mother Earth,' said Jo.

'Some people believe that Archangel Metatron was Enoch who is named in the Bible,' added Mariah.

Archangel Sandalphon

'Then there is Archangel Sandalphon, his colours are of the rainbow and he carries our prayers to Father God for us so that God can answer them. He is the Angel for music. He is guardian of Gaia Mother Earth and looks after the welfare of each of us.

In the early days it was believed that Sandalphon was the prophet Elijah in the Bible, but was then made Angelic. He is mentioned in lots of writings,' said Jo.

'So those are great Archangels. There are more but these are the most well known. They give off the love nature of our Creator God. They are the Great Beings of Light and have a bigger amount of 'God Essence' than we do, so you could say that we are small facets or little bright lights of these magnificent beings,' continued Jo.

'Now they are coming even closer to us and bringing their brilliance and their love and help to us. They are now letting us know about the world from where they come and what they do and they are now helping us to remember where we came from and the beautiful beings that we are and have been.

The Angels are now letting everyone know more about them than we knew in the past and those who want to can receive their gifts and their being there with us.

We can also call the Ascended Masters and any of the great Light Beings as well as the Archangels, whom ever feels right for us; we can ask them to over-light us,' added Mariah.

'It doesn't matter who we pray to or talk to Mariah, because if we don't know which Angel to ask for help with a problem or question, then they would know and so we could simply ask for the best Angel to help for that job, the appropriate Angel and they will help,' said Jo.

'Also the angels like simplicity and I like simplicity also,' said Mariah. 'I don't think we need to keep asking and asking over and over again for something. They can hear us and we could just trust that they have heard us and are helping us for our highest good.

We don't always see the bigger picture of our lives but they do and so they know how to best help when we ask. Therefore to ask for our highest good would be a good idea, and also for the highest good of others,' continued Mariah.

'They do love to help us Mariah, they are there waiting to be asked so they can help make us happy and to guide us in the right direction.

Sometimes if we are still with our thoughts we can get a 'bright idea' pop into our head, or sometimes if we think about something before we go to sleep and ask for help with this we could have the answer when we wake up in the morning when our mind is more relaxed and still.

If we are all the time worried about something our thoughts go round and round and we can't seem to get the answer or direction. If we trust it is so helpful and then we don't have to worry as we know that we are being helped and it will all turn out in a good way for us,' said Jo.

'Yes and to think of the good things and happy things, seems to make us receive more of the happy. If is like a circle, people that keep talking about unhappy things all the time appear to stay unhappy and the people that are positive, always talking about the bright side of life, they are happier.

So it seems to me that it is best to focus on the good and cheerful things and let the unhappy things pass by your thoughts without too much thought at all. There is so much beauty around us. Just look at nature Jo, see over there the tiny little creatures and the beauty of the flowers around the trees and the little winding path leading through the woods, they are positive happy thoughts.

Let's go for a walk down that path Jo and see where it leads. It's like a little magical pathway and I haven't been there before. I thought I saw a glimpse of a unicorn, maybe I was imagining, but it was over there behind the 'tall standing one', the tree. Look at all those trees in the background, the fruit is so big and bright and the ripples on the lake sparkle like little lights on the water,' said Mariah.

'I had a dream the other night Mariah; I dreamt that I was back in Atlantis. I could remember playing with a beautiful unicorn and her name was Snowy. She let me ride on her back and took me along a white glittering path by the stream. We came back past a beautiful waterfall and the water was gleaming and on each side were beautiful trees and exquisite red rock cliffs. As we rode along back the path we saw in the water a blue dolphin and this dolphin came up to the edge of the water to greet us. The dolphin was called 'Dolly' and she was very wise and I could hear her thoughts talking to me,' said Jo.

'Angels see everything from a higher place and they know that in the end we will all be taken up, and back to being the perfect little bright lights that we were in the beginning. They see our little bright light as when we came from the heart of our Creator as sparks of Divinity. The angels see only our beauty and they see us through eyes of love and want to help and guide us.

Some people have smaller sparks of light now though Mariah, as at this time of our lifetime on earth we have forgotten who we are and where we came from and some of us have not been so kind or loving as we could be. Not all of us of course, but some have changed for the worse over the years,' continued Jo.

'The Angels see all the difficulties some of us may have gone through during our lives and they understand that we need lots of love and help and they try their best.

As I mentioned earlier, when we are happy our Angels can come even closer to us. Their love is unconditional and so they do not judge us and their love is forever,' said Mariah.

'So we have God, our guardians and Archangels and all the wonderful Beings of light helping us all the time.

These days the Angels can connect with us through light. It is great to know that they can shine Angelic light over our shoulders to light up our pathway as we go along and soon we will learn how to do this with each other. The Angels say that this is called to 'overlight' us and then we will also be able to leave lovely little footsteps of light along our path as we go,' said Jo.

'That sounds amazing. We leave little footsteps of light all along the way as we walk by.

The Angels vibrate on a very high frequency of light. They are very beautiful beings of light and they are also messengers for us and I understand that the higher light beings have said they will soon show themselves to us,' said Maria.

'How is that,' asked Jo.

'Well some people can see Angels or patterns, but another example is that the Angels have been linking with some people that have been involved with the workings of digital cameras. The Angels have been helping get the vibration of the photos to reach the frequency of the Angels and other light beings so that their 'light bodies' can be seen on our cameras. That now means that sometimes we can see the beautiful beings with our own eyes,' replied Mariah.

'What would we see in the photo Mariah?' asked Jo.

'Sometimes in a photo if you look carefully you can see little white balls of shining light, or larger ones, like white balls; sometimes colours of blue or green or other colours. Many people are now seeing these Orbs of Light all over the world but don't always know what they are.

Many Light Beings came to earth aeons ago as Gaia was being made ready for us humans. They came in an Orb of Light then and now many of the great Light Beings are arriving from very far away universes to see the wonders that are about to happen on earth,' said Mariah.

'Oh yes, Mariah, we were talking about that in the other book about Lemuria and the Light Orbs that the Angels came in all those aeons ago, and the frequencies they brought with them from the heavenly realms,' said Jo.

'The Angels have said that they will be helping to make it easier for us to get nearer to them, and Jo, you can feel the Angels and Light Beings around when you have that lovely peaceful loving feeling. At those times when you are asking for help, saying prayers or your mind is still and you are thinking of them. Now there is a lot of bright light coming down from our Father God, down from the Great Central Sun and these times are going to change for the better for most people.

Mighty Archangel Michael has said that the Archangels are all that we here on earth are, but that they are also much more as well; that they are all the time in tune with our Creator and that the Will of the Archangels is in perfect harmony with Father God's will,' continued Jo.

'Yes Jo, and the love of the angels is always unconditional whereas our love can be conditional and judgmental sometimes. As well the angels do also love the loving energy that we send to them.

Our beautiful Archangels can create many wonderful things in a split second and as they are co-creators with Father God they all the time use their gifts for the greater good of all and also in perfect accord with Father God's plan. These loving angels particularly aspire to help and to guide each and every one of us during our journey towards our higher learning.

They have so much love and compassion for every one of us and they know very well and can appreciate all that we go through while we are here on earth with all our ups and downs. We have experienced life through the highs and lows and we have been hurt and fallen down and then we picked ourselves up again.

Our beautiful angels are there and they can only do something for us that is inside the universal laws and also when our will is in harmony with our Father God's will.

The archangels are not male or female though they can sometimes let us see them as either as they know what would feel most comfortable to us whether wings or no wings or as a light orb, or which would be the most suitable for us.

They do have their own particular way of doings things and they can be aware of thousands of us all at once and hear all of our prayers in an instant. They are mighty beings of light.

They see things from a higher place and so they know that in time we will all go back to our perfection, just as we were in the very beginning and we will be once more. They can see our bright or not so bright light and they know from our vibrations whether we are positive or negative, happy or sad; though they can connect with us more strongly when our aura is in harmony and we are at peace and happy. So if we can try and think in a positive way and be happy and look on the bright side, then life is easier for us in many ways,' said Mariah.

'I love the Angelic connection and of course there is no jealousy or 'put out feelings' among the rankings, e.g. guardian Angels and guides, as we are all one and they understand unconditional love and are happy for us to be happy in what we're doing no matter what. They all rejoice when we are happy and use our free will,' said Jo.

What is the order of the Higher Angelics Jo?'

The 1ˢᵗ sphere, and they serve as heavenly councils

Seraphim Angelics are around God to hold musical sounds to keep up the vibration of Creation.

The protectors of the celestial realms and stars and Angels of Wisdom are called the **Cherubim**.

Lady Gaia is a Throne for example, and so the **Thrones** are great beings of light who guard the planets. They are companion Angels of Planets,

The 2ⁿᵈ sphere—work as heavenly governors

The Angels of Mercy and the celestial prefects are called the **Dominions** and they govern the activities of the Angelic group lower than them.

The **Virtues** send out beams of light, Divine energy for us to be able to use more easily.

The Angels of Birth and Death and Lords of Karma, they are called the **Powers**. They are the keepers of earth history.

'Archangels are 8ᵗʰ from the top in the 3ʳᵈ sphere and here is the order, continued Jo.

3ʳᵈ Sphere—they are the Angelic heavenly messengers

Principalities—Guardians of every group, city and corporation and lots are involved in our planet here.

Archangels—Angels of Light who tend to the larger areas of human endeavour, they look after us all here on earth and the big jobs,' said Jo.

Jo then asked Mariah to remind her of the difference between intuition and inspiration.

'What is the difference between the two, Jo?'

Intuition

'I understand that INTUITION is information that we can understand straight away before we even think about it. Our Higher Self talks to us through our intuition and then this frees the way to our God Self, and then to wisdom from the cosmic records. It can also let us know by a feeling that something feels good, or true, or a frightening feeling when things are not right, and are not in line with the light or our truth. So is always good to listen to our feelings and act on them.

Inspiration

INSPIRATION is being inspired by something. This could be a thought that comes to us straight away, an idea that we get in an instant or something that we did not know before and then all of a sudden comes to our thoughts.

Sometimes we could receive a message from our angels and teachers to make us aware of things that we would not usually know about,' replied Mariah.

'So this means that intuition comes to my mind first and then from my heart, whereas inspiration will come through my heart first and then afterwards through my thinking. Thanks Mariah that has made it clearer for me,' said Jo.

'The times are getting exciting now Jo and all that we are hearing and learning. I am grateful to be here at this time in history to be able to experience all the wonders of the 'winds of change' coming towards the new Golden Age; and as well the Atlantean Angels are here on Great Mother Earth to look for people who will work with these angels and bring back the Atlantean energy.

Also, the great devic Angels and the faeries and elementals are helping with balancing and healing the elements here on earth and when Gaia is in balance once more there will be no more earthquakes or floods or other disasters because all will be becoming harmonious and then there will be a time of healing of learning and of love. Won't that be so wonderful to experience Jo?' said Mariah.

'Our beautiful Angels are here for us and to stir our hearts and encourage us, so all we have to do is to open our hearts so that these angels of light can come in and help us as they are always waiting to do. They are on the love vibration, their love is unconditional, they do not judge us at all and they only see our beauty and our light.

Some of us think by being martyrs we are doing good, by thinking of everyone else and forgetting about ourselves. Though we are equally important and we have to love ourselves as we do others. We do not need to martyr ourselves at all, because we are all precious and deserving of love. We are love itself and if we can give more love out to others then more love will be given to us.

Also we have our own Divine guidance for instance by listening to our feelings. Jesus once said to listen within. So we should do what feels right for us and go with that,' said Jo.

'The beautiful Archangels and Masters and other magnificent beings of light are working very hard with many people so that the truth and light will reach everyone as these beings love us more than we could know.

They all wish to see us share in Ascension at the close of 2012 because from that time it will be become similar to how it was over 12,000 years ago, before Atlantis fell and when Atlantis was in her Golden Age; a time of beauty and harmony and balance that we can hardly imagine just now in our limited form. Also we are loved so much by Gaia and nature, we do not realise just how much,' said Mariah.

'Those times were amazing Mariah, I have such memories about life there when we would dance and sing and everyone and everything was in harmony and surrounded by the beauty of nature and our little brother creatures.

Everything was fair and we learned by example. It was so delightful then and will be again,' said Jo as the two little bright lights sat out in nature admiring Gaia's beauty while visualizing and thinking about being in such a peaceful and enchanted 'heaven on earth' as it was back in the time of Atlantis.

Chapter 5

The Galactics

Jo and Mariah had seen this lovely planet with all her beauty and the chance to know what it would feel like to experience spiritual life while in the human body, where those living on Gaia could experience free will, emotions and feelings. These little bright lights would have a human body and would help build paradise on earth.

During Mariah's time spent on Gaia she always remembered when looking up into the sky, one very big bright star bigger than the others which was always there morning and nights. She loved to gaze at the brilliance of this star which always caught her eye. She stood gazing up at the shape of the moon on different nights and when it was a full moon she would look in amazement at the silvery brightness.

'Look at the sky Jo', isn't it so magical and pretty,' exclaimed Mariah full of wonder.

Other little souls wanted to spend some time in other worlds and galaxies. The planets and skies were so magnificent with their deep blue colours and millions upon millions of stars all sparkling like tiny glowing lights in the distance.

It was breathtaking to see all this beauty while they were Divine little sparks or souls and then they could venture on to other stars. It was joyous to be able to do this time after time throughout the ages and could continue to do so forever, travelling to different star systems and then back to the heart of Father God from where they first came.

Mariah and Jo had some wonderful adventures throughout the universe, travelling through time and space. Each time was a new story and always would be. Yes, they had very exciting and interesting ventures for two little bright lights as did all the other little bright lights.

Sometimes Mariah and Jo would meet up and other times they would like to travel to other planets as they were very inquisitive and wanted to experience all that they could. They always knew that they would be together at another time and could journey on, dancing and laughing in wonderment with their experiences; even when they were apart they would have very fond memories about their adventures.

They knew that the very beautiful and wise guardians and magnificent Angels and Archangels would look after them and help them during their life on beautiful mother earth and other places and sometimes they would be able to get guidance in those silent moments when they listened within.

Beautiful cool Central Sun

'There is a beautiful cool Central Sun around each hot sun, for instance Jo, it is above and underneath our own sun that we see. However the central sun is just so bright with light and no one can see it just yet. It is made from light from God and it is not hot like the sun that we know, or any other suns in other galaxies.

The big Central sun is very glorious and cool, not hot at all. We cannot imagine just how beautiful it is,' Mariah said to Jo. 'It is beautiful like all the other central suns.'

'It sounds such an amazing place.

'Yes, that is a place where the brilliant shining Divine bright Lights live. They were the first and the strongest bright lights that glowed from the heart of our Creator,' continued Mariah.

'So they would be the Archangels and the Guardians Mariah,' added Jo.

Pleiades

'I remember now,' Jo said. 'There is a beautiful place called Alcione which is the Great Central Sun of the Pleiades group. There are other central suns but this particular one is called Alcione and I would love to go there one day.'

'I also remember from our adventures eons ago when we knew such amazing things and I remember that Mother Earth and her solar system travel a very big path all around Alcione, an orbit of 26,000 years around Alcione in fact,' continued Jo.

'Thousands of years, that is a long time Jo, for Mother Earth and her solar system to circle all around Alcione!' exclaimed Mariah.

Arcturian Stargate

'There is a Stargate called the Arcturus Stargate in a higher place or dimension where there is so much light and it is like a gate to heaven,' said Mariah. 'At this stargate there are passages where people can choose which passage they want to go down and each wonderful passage would take them to a different place.

Remember Jo, how we would travel in Golden Atlantis; we would teleport in large and silent air-coaches. We needed only to imagine where we wanted to go to with our thoughts and we would be there.

Well you could use that as an example and when you get to the Stargate you could think of it as being a big air-bus station with big bright notices saying which direction the different airbuses are going to and a controller announcing over the loud speaker offering his help to the confused travellers. Some would announce 'last stop is Sirius', or 'last stop is Pleiades' or other such similar location,' said Mariah.

'Yes I understand that these passages leading to Sirius and other places are just so beautiful and it is from there that our spirit will once again alter how it looks and change into another form of life for the new experience that our soul would like to go on to. I wonder what form I would like to take when I leave there,' said Jo.

'So here at this passage we can make the decision as to what journey we would like to take and of course we would get lots of help as always from our Archangels and other loving Light Beings. We can meet up with lots of other beautiful individuals who might look different to us but this doesn't matter,' said Mariah. 'It is very exciting to meet all these different people coming and going to different places.

'I understand that we can stay a while if we wish, or we could go ahead and once again experience life in another place and learn about it. Perhaps we could go there together once again,' added Mariah.

'So many wonderful places to go to and continue to go on these adventures forever and then we return back to where we started with our Father God.'

'There is so much going on in the worlds and universes and all the magnificent Beings of Light. There is a beautiful group called the Council of Twelve which is the highest order in the universe.

Archangel Michael is from this Council and he comes to us to deliver messages of love, peace and wisdom. He also has representatives which are from the Galactic Federation who come back through time to give us positive messages. He is such a magnificent Light Being and from the 5th dimension where there is such a lot of beautiful light,' said Mariah.

Galactic Federation

'Ashtar is the top leader of the Galactic Federation and he works very close with the Angelic Kingdom and especially he works with the magnificent and mighty Archangel Michael who helps with protection. The Angelics and the Galactics work very closely with each other to help us all.

There is also another group called SaLuSa and they are from Sirius. They are also part of the Galactic Federation and they bring light to earth,' Jo responded.

'So we have God and all the wonderful Beings of Light helping us all the time while on earth or in other places. The Guardians and Archangels are there for us all the time and waiting for us to ask for their help,' said Mariah.

'Long ago an ancient people called the Mayans knew that the moon revolves around beautiful mother earth Gaia and they knew that Gaia moves around the sun. They also knew that the sun and all of the solar system orbits around the sun as well. The Mayans and other ancient people had lots of knowledge.

They knew that the sun and also the whole solar system moves around the Central Sun which is called Alcione and Alcione is the central sun of the Pleiades, and this orbit cycle is a Grand Cycle,' continued Mariah.

'How did they know all this hundreds of years ago', Jo wondered.

'Well the people from way back knew more than we do. They remembered more. They had advanced ways to build as you know from ruins around the world. They lived in harmony, they had special gifts and knowledge which they passed on and the Mayans had knowledge handed down from the Atlanteans,' Mariah reminded Jo.

Jo and Mariah had been there in Atlantis themselves, both in the times of Golden Atlantis and also hundreds of years later at the 'end times' of Atlantis when they had returned to help along with many others before Atlantis sank below the ocean.

Crystal Second Moon of Atlantis

Mariah was talking to Jo about a huge crystalline satellite: 'Remember the magnificent crystalline satellite called the Second Moon of Atlantis Jo? It was massive, about 5 miles long and round; that is really big. The Arcturians had come from their home planet very far away, they had come to build this satellite.

The scientist priest worked the satellite, but at the 'end times' in Atlantis before she sank below the Atlantic Ocean, he knew that this could not last much longer as the crystals and the crystalline grids for power were now under the control of the wrong people,' said Mariah.

The beautiful 'Moon of Atlantis' satellite had been there since the Golden Age and Mariah and Jo had been there also during that wonderful age to experience all of the beauty of this magnificent satellite which was made of crystal.

The crystals for healing and energy were controlled by this mighty satellite. They would send their crystal beams to the satellite and the satellite would act like a 'brain' and make better and clean the crystal beams. These rays were to help with agriculture, and among other uses they were also used for the healing temples.

The Second Moon satellite was just so beautiful it looked like a bright enormous moon in the sky and around it were rainbow colours spinning and glowing like pretty lights everywhere in the sky. Jo and Mariah were so happy to have been able to experience and see those wonders.

Then a scientist who came from Belial the destructive group, sent damaging beams to start earthquakes and to use against countries that did not do as they said. This was near the 'end times' of Atlantis over 12,000 years ago.

Beautiful 'Crystal Moon' lost some gravity and became weak; the power blacked out and no one could now rectify this.

'Fortunately our brothers from planet Sirius B help came to help just before the Crystal Moon crashed,' Mariah said.

'Yes, The Law of One and Atla-Ra who were the peaceful group, broke the connection and moved the energy crystals out of harm's way before it crashed. That was so sad at those 'end times' of Atlantis,' said Jo.

'I understand now though, this time in earth's history is such a very special period with happenings such as never before. That there will be lots of magnificent Avators sent to Gaia to show us direction and to overlight us.

We are so fortunate to be here at this time and to have the opportunity to experience the winds of change approaching the new golden times.

Gaia is only our home for a little while, whereas our family is from further away and the stars, the beautiful universes and endless amazing places from where we came, then further on from that the heart of our Creator,' said Mariah.

'Yes, remember Mariah, we have been such travellers; through space and time and seen the most magnificent sights and beauty along the way. We have been everywhere and done everything though we have forgotten the brilliance and just how beautiful we are.

We are going to see lots of changes while here on beautiful Gaia. Much of the old will be gone and the ones that stay will be different. We are going to learn how to be in a human body and yet still move in a beautiful light which has never happened before, this is completely new. The past wars as we have seen them will not be that way again and a whole new way of thinking and being aware, and everything we see will be so different and there will be peace and harmony,' said Jo.

Black hole

'I understand that just outside the Galactic Centre there is a black hole and in 2012 lots of energy coming from an advanced star group will come through the black hole into Galactic Centre to transform Mother Earth and the solar system, and the energy comes through the sun.

We will all have the opportunity to ascend and others will reincarnate elsewhere where the energies will be the same as their own,' said Mariah.

'Is that a case of light attracts light or dark attracts dark,' Jo responded.

'We will see with our own eyes a different new era and those people here on Gaia and also in other realms are working on this new age and as we said, some will be leaving and so those ones that will be staying will be different and it will be better for them.

We will learn how to walk in extra energy and light which is coming down to us and all this will happen while we are still in our human vessel and the things we will be able to do we would not think it could possibly happen, because this is something which our universe has never been through before,' said Mariah.

'Yes', said Jo, it is wonderful knowing about this special time in the earth's history with the earth rising to a higher frequency and that there will be many teachers and human guides as well as the Light beings to help us with the exciting changes.

They will help in a gentle and loving way so that we can adjust and move to a beautiful state of being. Some people here will stay, some will help from the heavens, some will return to the homeland where they came from or to another civilization elsewhere from the earth and some will return back to Mother Earth Gaia at another time when she is in her Golden Age.'

'I understand that some of us will meet our families from space and we will return home with them and as I have said,

I would love to return to Alcione,' said Jo as she had said on a few occasions.

'Gaia and all her loved ones who will be staying with her will rise in light and the people will be generous and peaceful and will have much honour. Things will be fair and we will be free.

I understand the people that do not want to have that type of life they will leave in the usual way when a person dies and leaves the earth and moves on, and they could return later while Gaia is in her Golden Age and they will be welcomed with open arms at that time by the loving people on Gaia,' continued Jo.

'We never die though Jo, we just change form and carry on our journey in another way; everything is like a circle, like the changing seasons,' Mariah responded.

Living in harmony

So the Winds of Change are coming Mariah. It will be so exciting to be living in harmony again as we have done in other Golden Ages or in other beautiful star systems during our journeys, and of course the perfection from where we came originally from the heart of our Father God Creator. The universes and all of God's creations are just so magnificent, look for instance at our beautiful sky at night, the bright stars, the beauty of Gaia and our little animals brothers and sisters, the elemental and plant kingdoms and also ourselves and our beautiful little bright lights within.

Though we have forgotten for now we will remember again the beauty of the other galaxies and star systems and the Great Central Sun. This special grand sun is cool and glorious and not hot like our sun. This is where the beautiful Archangels and Guardians and Bright beings of light reside and guide and help us and send their light and love and peace down to us. Yes there is so much beauty to be seen and to experience, we are only beginning and the beautiful thought is that it goes on forever. We make mistakes and learn but in the end we 'get it'. We remember who we are and where we came from and so our ways change.

Star Nation

'In our book about the Native American Lands, one of our brothers heard that "we came from the Star Nation and we will return",' said Mariah.

'It is going to be so exciting with the Winds of Change coming our way, responded Jo.

'Remember our wonderful journey in Arizona, some of the drawings on the rocks and mountains looked to us like spacemen, perhaps the people that drew them had seen some beings from another planet do you think Jo?'

'Yes, could be and many others think so. Also along another drive there more beautiful high red rocks and some more ancient drawings on them. You could try and imagine what the people of long ago were trying to tell us or what messages they were leaving us. We all tried to see what we thought they might mean,' replied Jo.

'As well, in southern Peru out in the desert there are ancient geoglyphs and they are known to people as the Nazca lines. There are straight lines and geometric shapes. Giant sketches drawn by the ancient people and covering a large area. They include figures of birds, fish, monkey, a human figure, an astronaut. As they are very large they can be seen best from higher up in an aeroplane.

There is a beautiful one of a hummingbird and many others and the geometry is very precise. There is also one of a man waving and his head which was an odd shape. Some people see him as a spaceman or the owl man, all very wonderful. Some say they are U.F.Os, some the theory of a giant astronomical calendar,' said Mariah.

The existence of extra-terrestrial life will soon become aware to us and there will be acceptance and a new way of feeling and thinking for us. Our brother and sisters from other places far away and also from other dimensions will walk among us in peace, harmony and love once again on our Great Mother Earth as it was many ages ago during the Golden Ages of Atlantis and Lemuria and before that, when our great Mother Earth was like 'Heaven on Earth', and we will all once again return to our former beauty and perfection,' said Jo.

'We have forgotten so much during the history of our beautiful planet Gaia, but I believe that we will know soon the answers to our questions. We will remember who we are and where we have come from and our glorious heritage. We will remember the beautiful bright lights that we are and of our magnificence and our long journey.

Chapter 6

On Native American Lands

The wonderful journey to Arizona in the United States was a journey that Marian and Jo would always remember. They set out from Sedona, a beautiful peaceful little place amongst all the wonderful red rock mountains, some nearby shaped like amazing monuments. The feeling and vision outside in the evening with the stars, the moon and the mountains are almost beyond description.

The mountains came in all shapes and sizes and looked even more beautiful than the background in many of the 'Cowboy and Indian' movies they had seen as children.

They were just so beautiful these red mountains and all the soil around was soft red. The pavements were also mixed with concrete and the red dust made into pretty pink coloured pavings for people to walk on. The roads also were red and the houses red or brownish and all blended in beautifully. The whole place was so clean and tidy and there were cute little pinky-mauve cactus plants everywhere.

These plants looked so beautiful and innocent, but not so!

'Look Mariah, these cactus plants looked like velvet, I touched them and they have left my hands full of tiny little prickles,' said Jo with her hand stinging in pain.

'They are beautiful though Jo. And last night I have never seen anything as beautiful as the sun setting down over those mountains. Mountains so different to anything I have seen in this life time, they are such different shapes and the red colour; a magical place to be.

The people are friendly and helpful and the shops are enchanting with crystals, beautiful plants and clothes. Also Native American shops with beautifully hand sewn gowns, boots, bags, musical leather instruments such as drums rattles, beads and feathers. I thought I was in another world or gone back to another time,' said Mariah.

Their story starts here in present times in Arizona, the great South West . . . .

'This beautiful land, I feel so still and peaceful being here and see the stunning red rock mountains and blue sky as far as you can see Jo, I have never seen anything quite like it before it is so magical. The scattered green bushes, the little mauve cactii, and houses the same colour as the pretty red pinkish land,' said Mariah as if in a dream. I can see why our Native American brothers chose to live nearby,' said Mariah.

'When Christopher Columbus found his way to America the Native Americans had already lived many generations in the South West and their ancestors before them had been hunters for their food and could make the clothes they wore. They became experts at growing corn and crops, and they survived well through all different types of weather and some of the land was very rough and some very beautiful. Some of the tribes were called the Navajo, Zuni, Apache, Hopi and many more brothers and sisters lived in different areas.'

'One thing I noticed Mariah, is that they have a wonderful love of nature, Mother Earth, Gaia. They were as one with the little creatures of the land and the trees they called 'the tall standing ones' and the woods and flowers, many that grew wild but beautiful. They were very much in touch with 'Mother Earth' and 'Father Sky; they called our Father God, the 'Great White Spirit' added Jo.

'The gifted first American people had weaved with wool after they had shorn the sheep. They would colour the wool with dye from the plants, they would spin and weave it and they made the most beautiful garments and decorated their blankets with love and skill which they could also sell for income for their families. These beautiful weavings were like treasures though, Mariah.'

'Also they weaved bright colourful baskets made from the willow and the yucca plants and as well as decoration these were very useful because food and water could be held in these baskets; they were sometimes sealed with a resin which was a liquid from the trees which acted as a glue to make the baskets waterproof; this resin could also be used to seal canoes. The baskets could be used in the ceremonies while the people were dancing and singing.' added Jo.

'I think the turquoise and opal jewellery is simply beautiful and other art they can create by hand,' said Mariah. 'The clothes are some of the prettiest I have seen, all hand made with beautiful blue and red stitching; and the moccasins, very soft leather, and feathers and beads in stunning and colourful designs.

The jewellery in the olden days was used for business and they would exchange one thing for another; the jewellery was made by melting old silver coins and hammering them down; some jewellery was made from shells and silver and stones and would tell a story by the pattern or design on it.

If the people were going through a hard time and needed some money for food and the essentials, they could loan out their jewellery and be given cash, then later on when they were able they could pay back the money and their jewellery would be given back to them again.'

Mariah had gone back in time in her mind:

'I can remember through dreams and distant memories of living in those times long, long ago and wearing all the beautiful soft leather garments and soft beaded moccasins, and in the winter we would rug up with fine-looking hand created blankets or coats lovingly made from wool and fur, and our were boots were laced up and very soft around our feet.

At night we would all sit around the fire, we would listen to stories from the elders; and as a very young child how loving and caring our brothers and sisters were. It was fun having all our families nearby and the elders taught us through their example of kindness; we loved to listen to the stories and teachings from our elders, the wise ones, with their smiling faces and sometimes very worn and wrinkled faces from many years of hard work and from the weather. I remember mothers would walk by with their little ones in cradle-boards wrapped and laced in, either on their backs or in their arms.

That was a happy experience Jo', said Mariah.

'It was fun to go down stream by canoe. I remember my canoe was made from birch bark and had blue and red paintwork zig-zagged along each side; on a calm day the nearby streams were like mirrors shining the pictures of the high mountains and tall trees, the 'tall standing ones'. They were happy days living out in nature with our beautiful animals to play with and the river nearby to swim and swing from the trees and jump into the clear water.'

'That was long ago though. Now we were in Arizona again, the great South West. It was like a land of magic and beauty.

Remember Mariah, the beautiful spot we had a lesson on how to do some painting. There was a beautiful area with a stream and rocks and further back the sparkling big waterfall; the water sparkled like a shower of tiny diamonds, it was so high the steep red rocks with hanging trees on each side; we tried to draw it with brush and paper as our Native American sister showed us how to mix and use the water colours amongst all the beauty of Gaia', said Jo.

'Then all the little lizards darting away as we walked by; I do remember though when I went up gently and said 'hello' to one tiny lizard that it just stayed still and looked at me, so I wonder if he could understand what I was saying and that I was not going to hurt him? He stayed there for a few minutes just looking at me and I was told that is quite unusual', replied Mariah.

'They would understand Mariah, thoughts are energy and they would know kindness and love and respond by not being frightened away and you were talking to them very kindly and softly.' said Jo.

'The woods were quite magical; we walked on through the trees and sat beside the rippling stream to listen to the water gently running over the rocks on its way down stream.

We saw some tiny fairies that day, hiding behind the trees. The fairies wanted to play and I felt as if they remembered us from somewhere. Their wings were like shining lace in pretty delicate colours, sometimes the little beings would fade or become misty and other times they were very clear to see; they were playing with us. Soon they came and sat beside us for a while joining us in laughter and then they danced off behind the trees again wanting us to go and look for them and to venture further into their enchanting woods with all the beauty of the great mother nature.

The next day we sat in a little clearing surrounded by trees and there were lots of rocks around but we knew that as it wasn't yet too hot we would be safe from the snakes, but we should still be careful when we walked around, careful of not disturbing the big rocks and staying in the clear areas.

Yes Jo, while we were sitting down I remember a beautiful blue humming bird surrounded us a few times, it then sat on a nearby branch as if watching and listening; then soon after it went around us again, so beautiful to see it there very still and observing us', said Mariah.

'When you are out with nature with nothing else to disturb you such as crowds of people or loud traffic and sirens, it is quite different and you can hear all the animal sounds and see them and realize how beautiful they are; 'living in the moment' and just watching what you are seeing in that instant, instead of as in the city where your thoughts can be a bit busy.

Hopi Mesa Village

We ventured on further with our Hopi sister and were invited and visited a Mesa and on to her village for lunch and to see how those kind people of the land lived their daily lives. They were very welcoming and we joined them for a meal of chilli beans, salad, flat bread and melon.

Many of the houses were very ancient and made of stone. They lived very quite simple lives and their families lived nearby, and they created beautiful carved and painted art work which they could use or sell.

We then joined the people at the Plaza, a square space surrounded by houses with flat topped roofs, to see a ceremonial dance and wasn't this was magical Mariah. The sounds were loud and very energetic and the dancing and chanting was marvellous to watch. The men folk were in traditional costumes, some with leather wrapped around their waist and leather moccasins and shakers in their hands; they had masks on their faces and over a hundred dancers went round in a circle, dancing steps forward, then taking steps back and making sounds and chanting as they went.

The people had gathered all around the side of the Plaza with their chairs and people also up on top of the house tops which were all flat; the houses were square and concrete or stone, very old and small and close together; there were ladders going up to the flat roof tops.

In a break between dances fruit would be passed around to everyone or thrown up on to the roof.

'Remember that event Jo, we climbed up the rackety thin ladder to get to the roof top overlooking the Plaza, we were very afraid though the local people seemed to do it with ease and kindly encouraged us; that was a wonderful experience to be up there and to see the dancing.

It was extremely hot though and we had our sun hats on, coming back down the ladder was worse and I was really afraid, but with help we managed to climb safely down the ladder and I was glad to be down,' said Mariah.

'We were lucky enough to see a few other ceremonial dances, but the Katsina dancers with their masks were very striking and colourful. Before they came out for their ceremonial dance they would wait a while underground where they dressed into their costumes and prepared themselves and this was in a round underground room called a Kiva; used for rituals by the Pueblo people.' Jo reminded Mariah.

'And also there are the Katsina dolls made from cottonwood roots, the plant and animal spirits are to teach the children to be good children, we were told.

The people from the Southwest dance to say 'thank you' for their food or if they have something to celebrate; they also dance a 'rain dance' if they want to ask for rain for their crops or dance to pray for the sick people.

These special dances are held in the winter time only and the snakes are asleep then also. This dance helps to remind everyone of the stories of old times and it is wonderful to know that these traditions are continuing, and I felt it was a privilege to be there to see this.' said Mariah.

On Navijo Lands

'Further on our journey and onto Navijo lands we were invited to a fire blessing, this was down steep in the rocks, though still very high up to see a fantastic view all around.

I was even more frightened than you were Mariah when we were all led down steep rocks by our Navajo leader; he said just hold on to my hand and come down. I took a deep breath and climbed down the rocks and you followed behind all the others.

That was a special experience sitting around the camp fire and ceremony with drums to connect with the ancestors', and also playing of the flute.' continued Mariah.

We shared in blessings and songs and a sweat lodge, which was like a steam bath in a tent and water was poured onto steaming hot rocks to make the steam; the rocks had been heated up outside over a fire. They were wonderful relaxing experiences.

'I had to come out earlier though.' said Jo. 'It was too hot for me I thought I would faint, but it was just so beautiful and quiet sitting outside the sweat lodge, seeing the magnificent scenery and the red lit sky while you were all inside.'

'Along the drive more beautiful high red rocks and some had ancient drawings on them, which you could try and imagine what the people of long ago were trying to tell us or what message they were leaving; we all tried to see what we thought they might mean, but people will probably never know what they exactly mean.

'Some of the drawings looked to me like spacemen, perhaps they had seen some beings from another planet do you think Mariah?'

A beautiful red canyon

'Next day after travelling further on, we went out on the land again. I did enjoy the walk down the beautiful steep canyon, and below was greenery and woods and a place for us to picnic. From the path at the top of the canyon we could see one part of the canyon had cows and horses below and that was a farm. The ancestors of the people lived there over 2000 years ago.

The beautiful magical Southwest of the great mother earth with her canyons which area so very deep and the mountains so steep; it surely is one of Gaia's most beauty and blessed lands, and how wonderful to live there all the time.

Then it was our solo night out in the open, so after getting prepared and some prayers, we got ready to sleep under the stars that night down in the canyon; my sleeping bag was not far from you. I could see you setting up your little sleeping area, and our other friends were also not far away; the reason was to stay awake all night and be quiet and at one with nature and everything, but not to be distracted by talking or being too close to each other' said Jo.

'That was such an amazing night. I heard wild horses running at one stage; it was so still though, and before the sun went down I looked around me and next to my sleeping bag on my left side was an area of woods, the trees 'tall standing ones' with all their growth and leaves at the top, and behind me and to each side in the distance were the beautiful high red rock mountains.

The beauty and stillness of the night

I lay there quietly just observing and taking in all the beauty and the stillness. The sun had gone down and I watched the big silvery moon between the trees, I saw it move through the trees and I wanted to see it come out from the woods into the open sky, but I fell asleep for a while before the moon came out past the woods' said Mariah.

'And lying there Mariah, I looked at the sky for a long time and it was full of thousands and thousands of big brilliant stars and they shone like diamonds against the deep blue sky. I have never seen such a magnificent display of stars before,' said Jo.

'That is because it is a natural place and not like a big city with lots of pollution, big buildings and smoke; here in this canyon it is fresh and clean and the sky is clear and you can see all of Mother Nature's glory and beauty. The moon and stars that night I will never forget' added Mariah.

'One of our friends sleeping out over the other side by the tall rocks said that during the night he heard a noise; he shone his torch and there were 4 little animals looking at him with wide eyes. They didn't come too close, just stood there and looked at him. He was a little afraid at first, but then realized that they were not there to harm him, they were just curious, and then went away.

Anyway I went to sleep peacefully, as we had all said our prayers and asked for protection and preparations the evening before and was lovely to wake up next morning to see the sun rising, to shake off our blankets and go to the have our breakfast cooked over the fire outdoors. The blue corn pancakes were delicious Mariah.'

The Southwest is magical, the land is so beautiful and the mountains and canyons so steep. I will always remember the beauty,' said Jo.

Medicine Wheel

'Down in the canyon later that morning we then experienced a 'Medicine Wheel' ceremony where you choose which of the four directions you want to lie, such as north, east, south or west because it has an important meaning, and so you decide which direction you want to be placed on the ground.

'Remember Jo, we were wrapped up in 2 blankets, very snug like a baby, and only our face was showing, almost like an Egyptian mummy. Then the others walked around us drumming and singing which felt very powerful and healing,' said Mariah.

Anasazi village

On our way back in a jeep we drove across beautiful white coloured sands that looked like rippled waves and not far away we could see built into the cliffs very ancient houses of the Anasazi.

The cliff dwellings were amazing to see and where people lived and left over a thousand years ago. The ancient people had built their homes high up in the cliffs and would have been the very earlier apartment type buildings.

The Anasazi were ancestors of the Pueblo people who dwelled up on the mesas and down in the canyons of the southwest hundreds of years ago.

Some of the valleys are pretty like a picture. They lie below the mountains and between and below each side of the steep cliffs there are small areas of green where the people can grow their beans and their corn.

Sometimes there will be a river running along the bottom of the cliff which will sparkle like little diamonds in the light of the sunshine; some of the mountain cliffs either side are so sheer and steep and all different sizes and patterns but often beautiful red in colour.

A Hogan

The Native American people have sacred or holy ways. They would for instance sprinkle corn pollen if they want to bless a Hogan. A Hogan is a Navijo house which is shaped round and has 6 or 8 corners to make up the circle and has a door which faces to the East. This is so they can see the first light of the morning sun, and a beautiful picture that would make, you wouldn't need to hang pictures on the wall.

'Our Navajo guide kindly took us to see his Hogan where he lived and to meet his family, and invited us to share a friendly meal of chilly beans, corn, steak and flat bread then taught us to dance out in the twilight of the evening,' said Mariah.

'Yes, they were gentle people, and we saw inside the Hogan, it had only earth on the ground with a little mat, with a window and 2 doors. One was to the east and when you looked outside in the distance it was so magical with the dark sky and sunset. When you looked out through the door on the other side of the Hogan the scenery was different but very beautiful and various colours in the sky of reds and pinks. You could not see prettier pictures,' Jo responded.

Our Navajo brother made us a sand painting on the earth floor, taking different coloured sands into his hands and sprinkling it slowly on the ground creating a beautiful design and this is to help sick people. Usually in a ceremony for someone who is ill then a Medicine Man will be there. It was a beautiful design and some Navijo artists will use these designs and sell their art,' said Mariah.

'As I mentioned earlier our Native American sisters are very gifted at weaving. They will sometimes kneel on the floor with their large weaving stand in front of them and after dying the wool from the sheep and spinning it they will weave it into the most beautiful crafted blankets or rugs and some of this they can sell to bring some income for their family.

The Navajo people tend to their sheep amongst the stunning monument valley. These magnificent red sandstone mountains are in various wonderful shapes like monuments and they are enormous just like some of the background in the western movies we saw as youngsters. The Navijo population is the biggest tribe in the land. Some live in Hogan houses and many of them on the farms and ride horses.

Many years ago they were hunters and they travelled far. Then about 700 years ago they decided to settle in the hills and way down in the canyons in the Southwest of America,' said Jo.

'Did you know that when Christopher Columbus arrived from Spain nearly 500 years ago he was really looking for India instead of America?' asked Mariah.

'Yes, but he accidently landed in the Caribbean waters and thinking he was in India they called the Native American people Indians and the name has always stayed with them, even though mostly they would prefer to be called the First Americans which they were, or would prefer to be called Native Americans,' replied Jo.

'The Government and Native Americans from the Southwest in the beginning met together in 'trading posts' which could also be used as banks or shops.

Code Talkers

Also did you know that the Navajo people were very helpful in the Second World War because they made up a special code in their own language so everyone could understand except the enemy.

This helped America to win the war and not a lot of people would have heard of that story. They were called code talkers and at that time their language had not been written but the code was extremely important to the USA winning in the Pacific during World War II. Some of the Navajo people could speak well in their own language as well as the English language and some of them were just lads who had made up the code.

One of the code words for example was 'iron fish' and this was the word for submarine and another Navajo word was 'our mother' and in code this meant America, and in the end there were hundreds of code talkers. They worked in several of the USA marines and fortunately the Japanese never did discover what the code words meant,' said Mariah.'

'Also Mariah, lots of the Native American people used their flutes to let everyone know that the war had ended and that there would be peace,' said Jo.

'I do love to hear the sound of the flute and I remember well our Guide on Navajo lands, sitting peacefully by the waters edge beside the beautiful woods. It was evening and we were getting our area ready for our overnight solo sleep out in nature. I heard the sound of the flute and looked ahead and saw this lonely silhouette figure in the distance and he looked so at one with great Mother Nature.

They are living between two worlds it seemed to me, our modern world with technology and eating some of our fatty foods, and also living the ways of their traditions using their long known skills and living in harmony with nature.

They have survived thousands of years living off the harsh lands of the Southwest and chose to remain there. They have remembered that Gaia fed them for all those years, before the days of the big shops and electricity.

Wisdom of the Elders

Our Mother Earth and every single creature are sacred to the Native American people. They believed that if we destroyed or ill used nature and her beauty would be to destroy life itself.

We did not understand these wise words then but now we understand the wisdom when we look around and see what we have done to our Mother Earth. So we must now do our best to change our ways and to think as the Native American people do, to see our beautiful Gaia as sacred,' added Jo.

'Yes and some of their ancient ways and knowledge of Mother Earth have been handed down from the elders to their children and their children's children, and there is so much to be taught and remembered about trying to live in harmony with nature and not destroying her. I hope that the sacred knowledge and wisdom passed down will not be forgotten and that people will live in harmony with Gaia and not continue to harm her,' said Mariah.

'Everyone prayed together for Mother Earth as she is 'crying out for help' and it is also good to send healing as a group and lots of people around the world are doing this now,' replied Jo.

'I agree, I think so more than ever now at these times.

Wasn't the journey to Arizona a beautiful journey Jo. The magical beauty of the Great South West, to remind us how to appreciate the magnificence of Gaia, her creatures, elementals and our brothers and sisters and to listen to the wisdom from the past,' Mariah had commented before she went off to her enchanted and magical garden amongst the birds and little creatures. She had lovely little separate gardens all with different flowers and plants and so could go from one to the other and breathe in the beauty, watching Zeta climb up the trees also called the 'tall standing ones'.

Zeta was her beautiful feline sister whose coat shone and felt like velvet, in colours of golden, white and black; she was like a miniature leopard. Zeta also loved the gardens, her wondrous territory and could wander endlessly into the different areas of beauty.

Both Jo and Zeta were at one with the great Mother Earth Gaia. They loved to spend as much time with her as possible as they did back in the times of Lemuria and Atlantis when it was like Heaven on Earth, and now with the 'winds of change' we are journeying towards the new Golden Age once again.

Our Mother Earth and every single creature are sacred to the Native American people. They believed that if we destroyed or ill used nature and her beauty would be to destroy life itself.

Aho.

Chapter 7

The New Golden Age

The perfect Golden Age has been and gone more than once and it is returning again and all of the great mother earth will be once again beautiful and full of bright shining light. Also the everlasting life in the solar systems has been and gone more than once.

We will be able to understand all this one day. It is like a circle, everything goes around like the seasons, everything is forever changing and will go on changing, round and round, coming and going and we will venture on.

Mariah and Jo had travelled the universes together and had been separated and returned together again to beautiful Mother Earth on numerous occasions. They had seen Great Mother Earth at her most beautiful when the people and all on earth lived in harmony and peace.

Though over the ages and eons of time many people had sunk lower in the third dimension and were not living in harmony any longer. They lived in fear; they had become greedy and were fearful of losing their wealth and their possessions. They had become powerful and were afraid of losing this power. They had lost their honour and many people thought only of themselves.

These people had lost their sense of fun and joy and forgotten how to love, how to live peacefully and to be in harmony with others and with the Great Mother Earth. They had forgotten how long ago they had loved to be out in nature with all her beauty and with her animals and the unconditional love that these sweet little creatures could give them in return for spending time with them.

Mariah and Jo could remember the times they had laughed with joy and danced and played with their beautiful companions; the little brothers and sisters along their way. They could remember the heights and the very depths of life at different times. They had experienced and learnt so much while in their life on earth and also experiences in other galaxies. It was wonderful to be able to do this time and time again throughout the ages and they could continue to do so forever.

'I would like to return again to Gaia for this special time of the new Golden Age. It will be a wonderful experience when Mother Earth and all upon her will be leaving behind all the sadness and darkness and ascending along with the Galaxy to higher dimensions. Also the beautiful energy of Atlantis will be returning to Gaia. I can remember the beauty of that era when it was like heaven on earth,' said Mariah.

. . . . **This is the story** of Mariah and Jo, two little bright lights and their journey towards the new golden age and the '**'Winds of Change'** about to come.

'I understand' said Jo, 'that end of December of 2012 is going to be a very special time indeed and the Archangels and the Ascended Masters wish to guide every one of us in our growth and to get us ready for the beautiful energies coming through in 2012.'

'Many of our ancient brothers and sisters from long ago knew about this date and this was very important for them to know, to remember and pass on this knowledge, and I understand that it is the end of a Mayan calendar,' said Mariah.

'The Mayans and the Hopi people as well as other peoples understand that we are coming to the end of a World Age and the elders from these two peoples do not prophesise that this date will be the end but instead they say that this will be a transition from one World Age to another World Age,' continued Mariah.

'Yes including the Maori people in New Zealand, the African and Native American people; so not just from one selected part of the world but from around the world they all knew about this. They knew that something was going to happen, a cleansing,' responded Jo.

'We are now in a purification stage and coming into a new cycle of energy in 2012 and so those around us won't influence us as much as previously.'

Galactic and Cosmic Centre

'Things are already starting with energies coming through and more energies coming later. There is expected to be a line up of planets, both Galactic and Cosmic Centre which is a first time on our Great Mother Earth. Sure, there have been line ups with Galactic, around every 13,000 years, but what is different this time is also the line up with Cosmic Centre because this has never happened before,' continued Jo.

'I understand that there is a black hole outside of Galactic Centre and energy will be fed into Galactic Centre in 2012 through the black hole coming from a superior group of stars, and the energy that comes through in December will change the world for the better, as well as the whole solar system; this energy comes through the sun,' continued Jo.

'I believe that this was planned long ago, many eons ago, even before the creation of our galaxy. There are amazing and beautiful energies coming through this gateway which we have not seen the like of before, so it is going to be something very amazing and wonderful that most of us would not be able to appreciate or understand right now though it will be made know to us so that we can all make informed decisions,' said Mariah.

'As we said before, also the Aztecs and other elders from long ago realized that something very important would be happening.

The ancient peoples could see that there would be a time when everything on earth would need to be purified because of all the damage people had caused to Gaia and because of all the negativity. Great Mother Earth is now crying out for help,' said Jo.

'Also', added Mariah, 'people will have a chance to become kinder people because of the planets making changes in their order. This alignment that you mentioned about the Galactic and Cosmic Centres and the very special energies coming down will make us more aware of how things are and help us to understand that which we don't understand right now.

There will be people who will decide to take on more light, to be brighter, and others even brighter still. They will be moving up to a higher dimension of more light. There will be more love in their hearts and they will want peace and harmony as it was back in the Golden Ages, and they were wonderful memories, Jo!'

'At this time I understand that many in the third dimension will move up into the fourth dimension of light, they will have more light, their hearts will open and they will be looking for peace.

Some of these kind people, and also children, special new children coming through, some already grown up, will help with the troubles of the world. There is a lot of greed and unfairness and this will be changed which is good, because people are becoming saddened with the ways of the world and feel inside themselves that they want a change for the better. There will be people to help others who may still not be quite aware of what is happening,' continued Mariah.

Cosmic energy

'I understand that there will be a fresh flow of cosmic energy to shine down upon Gaia earth and her people. This Divine light is from the Great Central Sun and will let us know that Gaia and her people are to move into the brighter light of the 5th dimension and the light will know what places it should go to,' added Jo.

'Of course there will be confusion and some people will suffer when the bright light from above hits some darkness and this will cause things to flare up; but coming from all of this many people will be brought closer together because it will open their hearts like in times of war or floods as we are seeing even now, and other disasters when people want to help each other and come together. I would say that we are seeing that confusion right now Jo.

There are big changes to come, life is shifting and we should let the old go. There will be changes on this planet. Things have to come to a conclusion like any cycle and as our cycle comes to an end something new is going to be born out of it; but when any cycle comes to an end there is chaos and confusion and that is what we are seeing now in the world. Something new is being born, something new and beautiful. A new way of being and we are part of that.

So things will be working as they should and will be one way that people will change for the better. The people with light and love in their hearts will rise even higher with this energy and light coming down from the heavens,' Mariah said.

'It will of course be time for some people to pass over and to leave great mother earth as always happens,' and I feel that when my time comes I would love to return to a planet called Alcione which is the Great Central Sun of the Pleiades group. I feel I have lived there before and would like to return and meet up with loved ones that I know have been with me all along, helping me in many ways,' said Jo.

'I think that I would be happy to stay longer if possible and help those that perhaps won't know what is happening and may be a bit confused.

I would also like to tell stories and tales of our past times together of the wonderful Golden Ages because knowing that will make people realise the beauty and harmony to come. To tell stories of all the fun and joy we had; dancing and playing out with nature and all the wonderful beings and little animals that came to play with us. In those days we could communicate with them by our thoughts as well as our words; it was wonderful wasn't it Jo?

'I remember you said that you and many others had stayed back at the 'end times' of Lemuria to help when their land went under the sea; to help them to safety across the land bridge and to the underground caverns,' said Mariah.

'Yes, they did try hard to save this beautiful land of Lemuria and all the people on her, though knew finally that it was hopeless. Some people went into the other realms in the higher dimensions of light and some went to other lands, then this beautiful Lemuria sank below the ocean with many of her people going down with her.

Many spiritual beings went to a place called Telos which was underground. They went from Lemuria across the land bridge and into the locks and caverns on to Telos which is at Mt Shasta in California. Mt Shasta is a very beautiful underground world of a higher dimension. These would be people of the bright light, and even today some people in the area say they have seen shining Beings walking out amongst nature and that they were wearing white tunics.

Other people went to Atlantis before Lemuria sank under the sea and they lived together with the gentle and caring Atlantean people as they were in those earlier days of Atlantis.

Later they were very clever with the material, machinery and technology and they became a more mental people. The Lemurians were artistic, loving and kind, and later on in Lemurian history had very advanced spiritual crystal technology. We have had much excitement talking about these wonderful experiences of Lemuria and Atlantis,' Jo responded.

'Do you think Jo, with the new Golden Age coming that it will all happen suddenly; that things will change in a big way?' Mariah asked.

'I believe things will happen little by little and already happening, but we will all know beforehand and so can make informed choices and decisions and we will have lots of help and guidance offered from our guardians and Angels and also from our human brothers and sisters and some earth angels,' replied Jo.

'I wonder how I can best help myself be ready in advance?' Mariah asked Jo.

'We could carry on living as peacefully and harmlessly as we can because then our energy light will be bright and it will help lift the energy of other people that we meet and help them to feel good and to learn by example. That is a good way to teach, by example as the elders taught in previous Golden Ages.

We could see all our brothers and sisters as we see ourselves. Also be kind to ourselves because we are just as important as others, and look after Gaia's beautiful little creatures and plants as they are all special too. We are all very special,' said Jo. 'We are all God's creations.'

Really we should just acknowledge God's love.

To chose love over fear

'There are two things and they are 'love and fear' which we can choose from. So to chose love would be the best way to go and know that we are all little bright lights, Divine sparks from the heart of our Creator and that our relationship with our Creator is so very important. To say some prayers or meditate, to think happy positive thoughts and enjoy the moment and have fun; these are a few things.

I remember this from how it was in Atlantis in the beautiful Golden Age,' replied Jo.

'I know what you mean Jo, to live in the moment as we did back in both Lemuria and Atlantis. Remember how we enjoyed playing with the animals out in nature, our unicorn Snowy and our dolphin Dolly and sometimes the fairies would join us in our 'hide and seek' games. We would ride or swim with them. We could also see beautiful shining Angels with their loving energy.

We surely lived in the moment then because it was so exciting and we didn't want to worry about the next day or the day before; it was all fun and joy. So yes I see what you mean Jo, to really enjoy the moment and appreciate those moments,' said Mariah.

'Another good idea is to do the things that we feel makes us excited and let other people do things in their own way, and not become controllers telling them what to do. We all have our own Divine guidance if we listen to our feelings and also Jesus said to listen within,' Jo added.

They both found their lifetime at present on earth had been quite different to life in the Golden Ages. However, their life had been good; they had also experienced the ups and downs of life this time and found that now in earth's history things have become less peaceful and not like it was in Golden Atlantis, or Golden Lemuria.

'Of course Mariah, there are people who have fun and happy lives, but there are a lot of unhappy people, just look around you. Many people have become greedy and controlling, so I wonder if in previous golden ages, when the times became darker and there was not much love around, people's hearts would be opened by tragedies as they would want to help each other and forget about themselves and their money,' said Jo.

'I expect some people don't want to change but many people feel that they would like change so they can live peacefully and have a world that is fair and happy,' added Mariah.

'I understand Mariah that things could start to go wrong around some of us and affect many people. Things aren't working out so well these days and there needs to be more love and so there will start to be changes for the best. With our free will we can decide how and what we wish to do. We will begin to feel more kindly towards each other and lots will be changing, even the people in charge of our country will be different and things will become honourable.

Unusual weather patterns

Mariah you notice the unusual weather, the colder or hotter seasons and more floods and disasters; Gaia is clearing herself and making herself new again through floods and earthquakes, getting free of negativity.

But I believe that we will all be in the right place at the right time and we will be guided; we are surrounded by beautiful guides and Angels and loving Beings of light and also wise and loving people who can help.

I understand that we will all know beforehand what is happening so that we can understand clearly and then decide what we want to do with these changes coming, the 'Winds of Change'!" said Jo.

'Also that many of us won't know what is going on and we will be given a 'gentle push' or supported and guided and we will be asking our Father God what is going on and will have the feeling to become closer. There will also be a human friend or guide to help us all on our way as some of these kind people will know ahead of time,' said Mariah.

'That there will be new people in charge so the world will be fairer and also a new kind of guidance for learning and 'teaching by example' as our teachers and elders did in Atlantis.

Remember how in the time of the Golden Age everyone was kind and gentle and we did learn by their example and we had lots of fun and laughter all the time.

So all will be well, it might not be easy for some people in the beginning but we will all be able to choose and it will be a great chance to remember our Creator,' continued Mariah.

'Our human bodies are slowly changing so that they can take more light coming through, the beautiful crystalline energy, our true essence, and we will know what is happening. There will be so much that will surprise us with all the changes.

Beautiful Light Beings

The beautiful Light Beings are working hard along with lots of people to bring the light and truth to each and every one of us as they love us so much and want to see us taking part in Ascension at the finish of 2012 and to begin to become as we were before Atlantis fell over 12,000 years ago. They also are helping stop the meddling of the people who are darker in their ways, the fearful and controlling people who have been powerful controllers for such a long time now.

There are now many beautiful Angels of Light coming to earth and many wise people will be here to help us with the 'Winds of Change.

Also Mariah, there have been and will be very special children and they are called the Indigo, the Rainbow, and the Crystal children and some of these children are here now and growing up and will be helping us,' said Jo. 'Some will be in leadership roles and will help bring about fairness us all, but we too can also help with the raising of our beautiful planet Mother Earth to that wonderful state of complete happiness and perfection once again, just as she was before in the previous Golden Ages,' said Jo.

We are like the tower of a radio station Mariah, we can send out and we can also receive way from out of space these new energies, and lately there have been beautiful energies that have been coming to earth and we are receiving more light and our bodies are changing. Also now many people feel that they want to be free, they are losing faith in the controllers and becoming tired of promises that never happen.

New cycle and shift

This new cycle and a shift is coming as we said Mariah, and it is called Ascension and also called 2012, and then further beyond, the new Golden Age. Very special energy is coming down from our Creator.

The old blocked energy of Gaia is being set free and because of this many people will change but yet there are some people that are still not quite ready to move further along at this time and so they could act really different to how they should or would usually act and this might not be very good. They might not be able to help themselves so they shouldn't be judged as we don't understand the whole story or the bigger picture but we could send prayers for them and their loved ones and not be judgmental.

'As you said Jo, something else we need to do for 2012 is to realize that Father God is our Creator and to acknowledge our Creator's love.

We will know well before the time what is happening and so we can choose up until the very last moment what we want to do. Father God is love and so he would not choose to have any of his creation suffer and we have free will we can choose what is that we want.

Footprints of Light

The energy that is very special will be coming down and it will come on down through us and then we will pass this energy out as if we are leaving footprints of light,' said Mariah.

'That sounds wonderful, leaving footprints of light as we walk along,' Jo responded.

'Also we should be confident with our positive thoughts and how we would like things to be, and as well if a lot of people come together in love they can rise above the negative vibrations of many people in the 3rd dimension. We are really strong and great Mother Earth has the story of the Lemurian Golden Age and the memories of that magnificent time. The beautiful new Golden Age in the future will be all the best times of the age of Mu, all the perfection and beauty.

'I understand Mariah that in the future there will be little light groups of people and certain people will be drawn to join them because they will feel comfortable and happy to be with them. Each person will know where to be and go. They will be at the right place at the right time because if it doesn't feel right to them then they won't want to be there. For instance people all wrapped up in their greed and all for themselves or violent people who want to remain in the 3rd dimension of the material, they wouldn't feel so comfortable with someone who is kind and sharing and not controlling so they would stay away and find themselves in a place they feel comfortable with other like minded people, as like attracts like,' said Jo.

'A way to explain the times ahead to others Jo, would be that in one way a new earth will be made and the old earth will change for the better; it will be transformed, and this is what many ancient people spoke of in some way.

It will be like God's hand coming down to end a time in the 'play' of life and people will know that something is going on. They may not know at first what it is and they will start to change their thinking and their ways. It will be like a beautiful flower opening her soft velvet petals and it's all going to plan,' said Mariah.

'Some people won't know what to do though Mariah, they won't know what is happening,' said Jo.

'Well there will be people there to help and to let them know what is occurring so they will understand also, though everyone will know ahead of time and be able to make their informed choices,' replied Mariah.

Who we truly are

'How wonderful that people will begin to live their lives in a way that they feel they are being true to themselves, who they truly are, and they will know what to do, ready for the next new Golden Age that is coming. This coming Golden Age will be like the beauty of Atlantis and Mu and will be the first time that people will be in the higher dimensions of more light and yet still remain in a human body, even though the body will look different to the way it looks now. It is slowly changing as we speak, ready to take in more of the crystalline light now available to us and continuing to do so,' continued Mariah.

'So as you were saying Mariah, it will be like the Golden Ages of Lemuria and Atlantis, when it was like heaven on earth and the people loved their lives and used their gifts and so were very contented. They danced and laughed and loved their loyal animal companions and enjoyed the beauty of nature and all her wonders. They were in harmony with everything,' said Jo.

'With the 'Winds of Change' that are coming some people won't even need to speak at all, they can just be a beautiful light and others will understand and then more people will start to hear and watch and know, and there will be teachers, there will be healers and there will be loving. It certainly will be a magnificent experience.

Returning to the Oneness

Another way which may help to explain Jo, is that everything is shifting and we are starting to understand and we will understand more. A very long cycle and darkness is now coming to a conclusion and everything is going back home towards the beautiful light. There are and will be wonderful energies coming down from both Galactic Centre and Cosmic Centre and we are all starting to return into the Oneness from where we came,' said Mariah.

'Moving into oneness, this would be similar to how it was back in Atlantis, where we knew that we were all one connected and that if we hurt another we would be hurting ourselves. Everyone was in harmony and loved their existence; it was one of our magnificent periods,' remembered Jo.

'Yes, and now this is everything in the whole of creation moving back into being ONE again; the planets, the galaxies, the star systems and all of us. The future certainly will be an amazing and exciting time and this time was chosen even before the creation of our beautiful galaxy and everything is going to plan.

These days most of us have forgotten that we could once take our body to another place in a moment. That we could travel to other places without transport and bring things to us by our thoughts as we did when we were in Atlantis. If we thought about an orange on a tree it would appear in our hands and all the wonderful things that we could do in that Golden Age. We have forgotten so much.

We have forgotten who we really are and where we have come from; the beautiful little bright light that came from the heart centre of our Father God.

We have forgotten all the amazing experiences and places that we have travelled to in the universe,' continued Jo.

'Though I understand that our memories will be coming back to us and we will know all this and the amazing thing is that this will be the very first time that people will be here in the higher dimension of the Angelic with more light and at the same time have a human body. That is so exciting Jo, and our bodies will change for the better and as well though we will be able to remember all the way back long ago.

'Yes we have journeyed through time and space to come here to have our experiences and to learn from them and then we move back through time again on our way back to Father God; that is certainly some journey!' replied Jo.

Lots hidden about past ages

'Yet during our journey here on earth lots of things have been hidden about how Atlantis fell after they left the Golden Age and sunk down in to the depths and things started to go wrong. There were many people from olden times, such as the Mayan people and their ancestors and other ancient ones who remembered Atlantis. They were people that lived in a very simple and happy way and they did not have the 'veil across their memory' in those times and they were able to remind people about Atlantis down through the ages, those that wanted to hear about it,' said Jo.

'So from now on Jo, we each have a choice and we will all know what we need to know for when the beautiful energies come through to us, and as you mentioned before some people will need help in remembering as they might not have had a chance to learn about these things but they will know, just as the people from Atlantis knew and the Mayans and other people knew,' said Mariah.

'But I understand that many will wish to stay at the stage where they are today as we all have free will. They may for instance be cruel and dishonest, greedy and controlling and not yet ready to receive the beautiful light energy and move on to higher and beautiful places.

They are trapped in the material world too much. People for instance who are too much living for themselves and do not want to listen and prefer to control. So these people could leave Mother Earth before hand as people usually do when they die and pass on but I understand they will know ahead and will have the choice to change their minds if they wish.

Also though there will be very loving beings who will also have chosen to leave before hand and perhaps give help from above. None of us understand the full picture but I understand that we will all be in the right place at the right time and will know,' Jo responded.

'Our loving Creator doesn't judge anyone because He respects that he has given us free will and of course at a later time when ready these people will be welcomed with open arms as they arrive back to a beautiful Golden Age or another place of beauty and have opportunities to grow and experience again. There will always be loving Beings to help them and when they are ready,' said Mariah.

'So if we can act in a loving way without judging, and recognise our beautiful Creator along with help from our Guardians and Beings of Light who love us dearly, all will be very well,' replied Jo.

Wonderland of harmony and beauty

'Yes, and after some upheavals for some and a little more awareness for others and some changes, the future will be like a grand fairy story with a wonderful happy ending for those that choose love. It will be like going to sleep and waking up in a wonderland of beauty and harmony with all the heaviness and unhappiness that we have been carrying through this lifetime being lifted away from us,' said Mariah.

'I understand that the whole planet is due to awaken; that the future cities will be different to how they are now, and to enable us to understand how a town or a city can be more like Paradise we will work with our children to know about this. Much like being back to Lemuria or Atlantis in those wonderful times and the way things were then. This vibration has been re-activated here on Gaia and there will be shifts and changes to become Paradise once more.

We should live from our hearts rather than our heads, and follow our intuitions and feelings so we find our own truth. To listen to beautiful Gaia Mother Earth and to see her beauty and of course make time to dance and sing, to be joyful and to be creative,' said Jo.

Mariah and Jo were remembering their wonderful journey in Arizona and some very wise words they heard so simple for young or old to understand and summed up some things that they had been talking about on the New Golden Age.

'Life is shifting,' said our wise and beautiful sister, 'there are big changes to come and we should let the old go. A new tree cannot be born unless an old tree dies. The new tree feeds on the old tree for life. There will be changes in this world; things have to come to a conclusion. It is a cycle, like any cycle. So as one cycles come to an end something new is going to be born out of it and when any cycle comes to an end there is chaos and confusion. That is what we are seeing in the world; all that confusion out there in the world is coming to a conclusion and something new is being born right under our noses, something new and beautiful. A new way of being and we are part of that.

So we just have to keep focused on beauty, on goodness and love and bring to a balance, because this darkness has got well out of balance and the Navijo talk about the beauty way, it is a way—beauty in our speech, beauty in our home, beauty surrounds us, and as we are that way we are beauty from the inside out. Some have lost their way and you don't see the beauty any more because they have been beaten down by the world, but those that are really living it you will see a radiance of beauty that comes from them and you can see—"that's it— he knows the way!"

'That sounds very good to hear said Jo.' Was there anything else she said to you?

'Yes, the more you stay in this moment, right now, the easier you will fall into the 4th and 5th dimension. It may feel like you are losing your mind; that part of your mind that is leaving—just laugh and say to yourself: "Just because I am losing my mind, I can't remember where my shoes are, or what I did yesterday; it is OK." And have fun with this change and shift. If money goes, it goes.

We know how to live without money. We know how to do this and we can barter and somebody is good about story telling; hey, we will give you some grapes for that or somebody may need another car. I will gather all my art work—will that be OK? We will make a trade so whatever we have we are going to start trading.

But don't fear because it is like the old tree goes down and the new tree comes up and always lives on the nourishment of the new tree—you see in the forest the new tree comes up where the old tree dies because it is feeding on the old, and the old tree says: "Here honey, I am going, this is for you," and we see something new.'

'Those are beautiful words Mariah, said Jo.'

'So Jo, when in the times ahead if we should see some turmoil and difficult times we should try hard not to think dark thoughts, but we could instead see a beautiful place and create it by our beautiful thoughts; to think about the beauty of the land, the cute loving animals and the diamond light sparkling on the water with the reflection of the moon, the beautiful 'tall standing ones' called the trees.

We could see a beautiful picture of everything and of our brothers and sisters living in harmony and love all around us once again and to feel that we are at one with our Father God and all of God's creation. We could remember the beauty of those golden times of Lemuria and Atlantis, when it was like heaven on earth,' said Mariah before she fell asleep in her garden in her beautiful natural surroundings. She had always loved to be amongst nature and to be able to still her mind for a while, to be with the wonder and beauty of Gaia.

Her beautiful feline sister, Squeek with her black shiny ebony fur was always waiting to give her unconditional love; she placed her paw into Mariah's hand and rested her head on her arm.

Jo liked to day-dream and to feel the energies from this peaceful place, she watched the trees dance in the gentle breeze and was aware of the pale colour of pink across the blue of the sky; she loved to visualize what it might be like in the new Golden Age.

Chapter 8

Create your World

Dream big and reach for the stars and remember that we will experience those things that we create with our thoughts, so let's once more as in the previous Golden Ages, create a beautiful paradise on earth with love and harmony.

Dream big, dream really big and let your imagination go wild, because the wilder it is the more truth there is in it. Even if you create in your imagination, a fairy land or a world that is bountiful with trees, big huge grapes on the vine, apples that are this big!

So dream big, imagine big, because as you do you will imagine a place for the animals now to live on the land that is wonderful. The oceans are filled with sparkling diamonds in the water that glow at night, a garden which is magical, trees 'the tall standing ones' that are so tall and straight and special. As you tune into all these things and ask for what we need, let your imagination run wild.

. . . . This is a story about Mariah and Jo, two little bright lights or twin flames who eons ago, came from the heart of our Father God.

'It is a story about my dream coming true, a dream about creating my abundance, the process and the result,' Jo had written in a letter to Mariah.

'In the autumn of 2006 I made known my intentions that when my creation of abundance came forth as had other creations manifested for me in the past, I would have the evidence to write about much of the knowledge and insight I had gathered over the past 30 years, especially the last two years. This would all be worth writing about and a reminder that it is in fact possible to have that which we choose to have in life. I would like to write in simple terms about creating abundance because I had experienced this first hand and had the proof' Jo wrote to Mariah.

Jo did not in fact write the book though she left it for Mariah to write about in one of her books because Jo found that her manifestations had come about over the years and many of her dreams had come true. Perhaps not at the time she would have liked, but we understand that could also be 'Divine Timing', a perfect time for us when all involved works out perfectly and a time that we might not see the big picture but we do later on.

Jo had written a vision board on which she put pictures and photos of her dreams and then she put it away, looking it from time to time. There were times when she thought none of her dreams would come about but she quickly put those thoughts out of her mind and would continue to dream about that which she chose to happen in her life.

Jo had been a fashion designer by profession, starting with the fundamentals as a young girl, learning over many years every aspect of her profession to the time where she owned design labels, with the business and clients in two countries. Spirituality was always there in the back of her mind waiting to become prominent again when there were times of less pressure. She was later determined to make time.

Wonderful experiences

'I found on one occasion Mariah, that when I had been taken ill with flu and forced to stay in bed for a week, I had a few wonderful experiences. My mind was completely relaxed due to the fact I was not well enough to do other than lay in bed. I was alone at home in quietness. I had meditated and watched or listened to spiritual videos. I found soon that my severe skin rash on my hand had completely disappeared.

Thoughts and ideas were coming to my mind which would make a turn of events and career,' wrote Jo, as at that time they corresponded my mail as they both lived in opposite sides of the world and met up yearly when their families came together.

'This was not an easy decision to make,' continued Jo in her letter, 'but my passion for the spiritual path guided me followed by the knowledge and experiences I was having, as a consequence of having this quiet time to be still and to listen. It felt as though my consciousness had been raised,' Jo was telling Mariah when they were together.

'I wanted to become 100% focused on creating my desires because once these come into my reality I could have the book written and how exciting to think of all the creations that would follow next.

As we were educated in an orthodox religious school one might presume it unlikely I should happen upon such readings which came 'outside the box; however as long as I could remember I had a passion for spiritual books and metaphysics, the last two years concentrating mainly on creating.

I meditated often and enjoyed working with Angels and Archangels. Having learnt about Angels at school we both had a renewed interest came about quite suddenly, and not co-incidentally I feel.

Remember Mariah while on your trip home we were seated at the computer and out of the blue an Angel and Archangel Website suddenly appeared of its own accord changing from a completely different website,' continued Jo.

'Yes, I remember that day well. We were sat in front of the television screen together. We had gone to the website to call up a subject, completely different to what appeared on the screen, and now on the screen appeared the site of Angels and Archangels, pages and pages. Remember Jo, we sat in front of the screen all day, stopping sometimes for a cold drink. We remembered some of our school teachings and learnt so much more, we were so very interested in all the information and learning that was coming to us about the beautiful Angels and Archangels,' said Mariah.

Ever since that day both Mariah and Jo had become so very interested in knowing and learning about these beautiful Beings of Light. Their Guardians Angels and Archangels had become a part of their every day lives.

'I often ask my angels for a parking space and mostly it happens, I ask for help in so many ways and always receive help, said Jo.

'You read many books didn't you Jo, in fact we both did. I remember you telling me that in your youth you began meditating and had met with like minded friends,' said Mariah.

'Yes, and also I remember that I began listening to CDs and cassettes on spiritual matters and metaphysics and when I thought I had found the best there could be, something more profound and beautiful always came along,' said Jo.

'It was in 2004 that I came upon some wonderful spiritual material on the subject of creating one's own abundance; visualising and focusing on dreams and creating these dreams. The various types of material constantly appeared as if purposely and the more I learnt and meditated the more excited I became.

I was very aware of synchronicities taking place; more information was coming. I decided to focus solely on creating my abundance, all the while jotting down the exciting knowledge and ideas which came to me,' wrote Jo.

'This was the time I decided that when my creations of abundance materialised I would write about the process of my thought creation, my focusing on that which I wished to have and knowing and giving thanks, knowing that it would come to me. I thought that this would be a book wherein I could speak clearly, simply and repeatedly about creating abundance, having experienced this first hand.

I continued jotting notes in my journal notebook, my thoughts, incidents and conversations. There was so much wisdom and inspiration from different writers and channels or from within during those quiet still moments of listening. I didn't realise then that it would be you that would write these experiences for me,' said Jo.

'Those early dreams and your hard work would have been the results of your passion at a young age to become a designer which had taken many years. Your focused thoughts and going to college and dreaming about becoming a designer had actually come about and your dream came true by the creation of your positive thoughts and I also remember that you were always thankful,' said Mariah.

'Yes, and towards the end of my career, I realised that there was and had always been within me, a desire to work in a spiritual way. For instance healing work and perhaps automatic writing, I was not sure, but knew that I was being drawn to another type of work,' said Jo.

Now subsequently in life with my learning and spiritual knowledge, I awaited my desired creation to come in more quickly, to manifest, through my focusing on my imaginings or dreams, my strong emotions and my staying on the happy and wellbeing vibration.

On a morning in October 2006 I had been creating my day; I did this religiously before I was fully awake. This day I was in my warm bed reading and listening to works on abundance and also my intuition, which I did every few weeks as it kept me in practice of my thoughts.

Feeling really focused and with monitoring my thoughts and emotions, and with practice, it was becoming easier to stay on the happy vibration to bring my desires into manifestation.

I was just thinking how marvellous it would be to write a book on how we can create whatever we want, with proof!

I had no intentions of giving up this focus; it was only getting stronger and stronger.

I was continually entering into my notebook,' wrote Jo to Mariah.

'Miracles can happen and it's so simple' all I need do is notice my emotions. When I feel good I know I'm on the vibration of Source (God) or when I feel not so good I'm on a different vibration. The beauty of it is that I can change my mind at a moment's notice. All I need do is think of anything that makes me feel good. Or I can just clap my hands to put a smile on my face.

When I'm happy and draw my attention to yes and that which I wish to have, this abundance comes to me. When I'm unhappy and draw my attention to no, and to that which I wish not to have, that comes to me also. If someone should speak to me in an unpleasant manner I can simply change the subject or walk away,' wrote Jo to Mariah.

'The information I was learning through reading and listening really made sense.

'I prefer simplicity and I now know this is sufficient. All you have to do is notice your emotions, when you feel good you are on the vibration of source (God) the love vibration; when you feel not so good you are on a different vibration.

There are two vibrations and if you are aware of them you can change at a moment's notice,' continued Jo.

'All you do is think of something—anything—that makes you feel good. Past is past, some like to call in Archangel Michael to cut negative cords; though you can just think happy thoughts and you can bounce back to source vibration which is who we really are.

If you find that hard to start with, just clap your hands an Angel reader had said; that puts a smile on your face and you straight away feel good,' said Jo towards the end of the letter.

'I did love receiving your letters,' said Mariah. 'Here is more than you wrote to me during that time Jo.'

"I could see with my every day practising that it became easier and easier because the more I practiced the more I became aware of my emotions. Emotions are the tool we brought forth with us to keep us on the source vibration of who we are (Source). This is when miracles happen and all our wishes manifest.

When we slip off this vibration we push away our asking—for whatever we want or think of. We are creating every second of every day, whether on a good or a not so good vibration. This is why mediums can not often accurately read our future as we can change our path, whether we are aware of it or not, at a moments notice because we have free will,' wrote Jo.

'I understand Jo, that we have a probable path that we chose to walk, but that because of our free will we can change this. But we always have the guidance and can listen within and our feelings will let us know also. If we feel happy and it feels good, then we would be on the right path,' said Mariah.

'I was so excited about having this knowledge as it was so amazing to be aware of my emotions and thoughts and I am finding I am aware of these more and more.

What could be better than learning to think happy thoughts most of the time, to do things the way that excites me. If there is someone that is not pleasing or talking in a way that is not pleasing, I can just move away or change the subject. I was getting skilful at this now.

If a person is being negative I could ask, "How are your emotions feeling now?" and they would realise. But if it is a bigger issue, say at work for example, I would say to myself,

"I'm moving away, I'm not letting this change my emotions," and walk away,' wrote Jo.

'Draw your attention to <u>Yes</u> (things you like) it comes in. Draw your attention to <u>No</u> (things you don't like) it comes in. <u>Do not</u> draw attention and it will not be included. (All thoughts count whether the thoughts are of past, present or future).

'Relaxed in my room the rain fell and I could hear the drops dancing on the roof and felt the beauty and calm within. From the space within I focused patiently awaiting my desired creation. My visualisations, my dreams at night were lovely. Becoming ever clearer I could feel them with my emotions. Monitoring my emotions developed easier with practice allowing me to stay on the happy well being vibration, a wonderful way to think.

I looked at every day differently now, inviting into my space only that which was positive. I felt a difference in health and energy levels, a wonderful way to feel,' continued Jo.

'I remember we would both write on paper, words about how we would like to create our day, all the things that we would like to draw to ourselves, for example on that day we would like wealth or abundance or energy, and say those words, or change the wording as we chose,' said Mariah.

'In January of 2007 I told you Mariah that I was visualising a big win in the lottery and was going strong on the other visualisation, the retreat and then the book. I felt I was on the well being vibration, practice makes perfect I had said. I handed over any problems, was doing so daily and enjoying every day. It wouldn't be long now, I felt abundance was coming to me and was enjoying the process.

A few nights later I woke up, someone was calling my name. The voice woke me, then I heard it again. I thought it must be my husband who perhaps gone downstairs, but no he was fast asleep and when I looked at the clock I saw that it was 3.00 a.m. I wondered who it could be, was it mum? the Angels? It certainly was clear.

9.00 pm was my favourite time of the day, Angel card readings, meditations, visualisations. I felt I could do this all day if there were the time.

Every month I was in the lottery draw for a beautiful home in Australia. The new house in the draw was as lovely as the last and of course I could go through every room with my eyes shut visualising the house, I loved it. This I wished to have for my place of work and spiritual retreat,' continued Jo.

'Well you didn't win at the Casino in Los Angeles or win the lovely house in Australia; however better still your dreams and visualisations did come true I feel Jo, because you did get your beautiful home and have a magnificent healing room which I call a retreat, though you still want a bigger retreat. Your healing studio has a beautiful atmosphere and you have all your angel pictures and statues and crystals and so many beautiful Angelic and spiritual pieces you had kept for years in your attic in your previous home and now they have found their place where everyone that comes for healing can see.

People that come for healing return and recommend others, so your dream or visualisation of being a healer has eventuated,' said Mariah.

Home on the Hill

'Your new beautiful home which is surrounded by all the beauty of Mother Nature and bush lands and flowers came about quite strangely didn't it Jo. Once more, when lying in bed you heard a name calling, you got up and went straight to the computer at 4.00 a.m. in the morning. You and Will had both been looking for a home for a long while after selling the business. It took nearly a year and you had been let down as things weren't working out that year.

However this particular morning when you went to the computer there on the screen was a home and you were drawn to it immediately. You both waited patiently for the estate agent to open office so you could see this house and soon this home was yours, everything you had visualised, up on a hill, surrounded by beauty, your healing studio outside.

It took a while and you had been let down, but I feel Jo that this may be to do with 'Divine Timing' as some of the previous homes you looked at and were not able to purchase, you realised later that they would not have been suitable for you anyway.

Here was your perfect home, surrounded by nature and you had your perfect place for your healing work. I bet you couldn't believe how this had all unfolded and I remember that all the while through all the difficult times of that year you hadn't lost faith and had kept strong with your visualisations and dreams and eventually when the time was right there it was.

It wasn't the lottery home in Australia, where it probably would have been too hot for you anyway, but it was as you really chose to have.

So we don't know Jo how the process of getting our dreams will unfold. We ask and give thanks for that which we would like to have but for the end result, we don't need to concern ourselves about the way that it comes to us. How long it takes could depend on Divine Timing, or as you said earlier perhaps a person's thoughts may not be on the right vibration, perhaps there could be negativity in someone's thoughts to delay things or they are dwelling too much on what they don't wish to have, rather than focusing on the things that they do wish to have. Because as you said if you draw your attention to <u>Yes</u> (the things you would like to have) it comes in. If you draw your attention to <u>No</u> (the things that you don't like to have) it comes in. <u>Do not</u> draw attention and it will not be included. (Every thought counts whether thoughts are of the past, present or the future).

It has worked for you Jo, and also working for me, because I have for many years been writing and saving my works on the Golden Ages and the Angelics etc., not really knowing why, other than that I enjoyed doing it with a passion. Then one day while I was quiet and listening to the wind I had the sudden urge to write books, to get everything set out in a certain way and to have them published. For years though I didn't know why I was doing this, why I was writing, so either it was something I had visualised earlier or it could be a path that I had chosen before I came here,' said Mariah.

Mariah and Jo were on the plane remembering their journey in Los Angeles and now on their way to Auckland to see family. 'You would think that we were millionaires wouldn't you Jo,' said Mariah.

'Money doesn't have everything to do with it. You've heard of Abundance Consciousness haven't you?' asked Jo.

'Yes, and I can think of an example of positive thought creating that which I would like to have. When I think and dream about my holidays during the year they always eventuate, even though I may not have the money at the time of the initial thought. The work is always there for me and that's the way it has always been with my travelling since the age of 21. I always trusted that I would be going on holiday when I chose,' replied Mariah.

Abundance and poverty consciousness

Jo added that there was abundance consciousness and on the other side of the coin there is poverty consciousness.

'Whatever thoughts you focus on clearly and passionately, the universe will say 'yes' and present this to you. You don't even have to think about how it will be delivered and money doesn't have to be the deciding factor. Take what you do Mariah, you decide that you will take your next trip, knowing at the time you may not have the money presently, but you go ahead anyway with plans and your trip falls into place. I remember how positive you always are when you leave Auckland, you say that you don't have a job to go back to as you work for an agency, but you know you will have a job,' said Jo.

'That's right, and I always do. I know people who stay in jobs they hate, you hear them say they won't get another job, they are too old, not qualified or other negative thoughts they can say to prevent them getting the job. As you said, the universe answers 'yes' to them. It's important to watch what you say after you say the words 'I' and 'I am' for instance I am rich or I am poor, or I will never be rich or I don't want to be poor. We should always use positive words, and not words such as 'I am poor' or 'I won't get a job' because if we say these words and keep talking about it repeatedly that is what could manifest,' said Mariah.

'If someone says constantly and puts feeling into it, 'I am poor' or I won't get that job', the Universe answers with its only response which is 'yes'. That is what we will receive. If we keep changing our mind, the Universe—God or Angels will be bringing something to us that we are focusing on, then we change our mind and it gets taken away. We have free will and it is up to us to choose our creations and we are creating every minute of the day with our thoughts, whether they are positive or negative,' continued Mariah.

'I too believe that by following my passion the required means will come about. I don't have to worry about the end result or how it will materialise, just that it is what I wish to have, focus on what I desire, not on what I don't want. Whatever I focus on will come about, so if I think about scarcity, it will increase and materialise and if I think about abundance, it will increase,' Jo responded.

'When I ask I know to be specific about what I choose to have and know that I am worthy to receive it and that it be for the highest good of all. I don't worry about the end result because it could arrive in a way in which I least expect, but I don't mind being surprised. There could be a delay as you have experienced Mariah, and I think that would be Divine Timing, which is to do with working out perfectly for all concerned. Importantly I would say 'thank you', because even before I have received it I trust that it is coming.

I like to lie back in bed sometimes and think about all the beauty and surroundings and sometimes I see myself running along the beach in the waves very fit and healthy and laughing. That reminds me about our journey in Atlantis Mariah, the way we would laugh and play and splash about in the water with our lovely dolphins,' said Mariah.

'Yes, those were such wonderful times and of course will be again Mariah. I also believe that gratitude is very important, the more grateful we are the more we receive. There is much to be grateful about if we but look around in a positive way and enjoy the moment, because complaining puts a grey mist around us making it difficult for Angels and loved ones to get close to us and help.

It is a great idea to stop reacting to our past situations and all the time repeating the same scenarios over again when we really feel we would like to do something else. It is also great that we can create something brand new by our focused thoughts and we will be happier and have more energy because we are doing that which we enjoy rather than the things we don't want to be doing. It's a lovely thought Mariah that we can make a fresh start by choosing to do so by our thoughts and the way we act,' said Jo.

'It seems, that I actually do focus on my desires automatically by remembering the feeling of happy events, holidays, thanksgiving and frequenting Italian and other enjoyable restaurants and beautiful places and I really do appreciate it all and enjoy every moment,' said Mariah.

She remembered another example of money coming just at the right time, a few years back when their mum and dad's car was permanently out of action and their brother had phoned wondering if they could all contribute to buy a new car.

'Yes I can help' not knowing where the money would come from, though soon after putting down the phone she noticed on the kitchen bench her tax rebate cheque for almost the amount that she wanted to contribute to the car.

While she knew she didn't have the money herself right at that time, she had the faith that the money would be available and she wanted to give this money out of love and to help with the car and there it was in the form of a rebate cheque.

Mariah while tidying up then noticed on the bench the letter she had received from Jo and along with other news, reminded her again:

'Miracles can happen,' wrote Jo, 'and it's so simple, I have only to become aware of my emotions.

When I am feeling good I am on the Source (God) vibration and when I am feeling not so good I am on another vibration. The great thing is that I can change my mind at any specific moment.

When I am happy and think "Yes, that is what I wish to have", the abundance will come to me. When I am unhappy and think "no, that is what I chose not to have", and continue thinking about these things that I don't wish to have, they will come to me because I am focusing on them a lot and putting a lot of energy to it. If someone speaks unkindly to me I can either walk away or talk about something else, I can change the subject, I don't have to buy into their negativity.'

If I draw my attention to Yes and to that which I would like, it comes in, however if I draw my attention to No and those things I would not like, it comes in. If I don't think about it, then it won't be included. All thoughts count whether they are of past, present or future.

If I am aware of my thoughts I can change them at a moment's notice; all I do is think of something, anything that makes me feel good.

The past has gone, you can call in Archangel Michael to cut negative cords if you wish, or you can think happy thoughts again and you can bounce back to Source vibration,' wrote Jo.

'On the other hand' said Mariah, 'poverty consciousness could be to do with your way of thinking, the way you have been brought up and what you have learned from your family and environment and your thoughts and fears of not having enough of anything. It depends on how you feel inside and your mentality. You could for instance be disadvantaged or perhaps a homeless person but that wouldn't necessarily mean that you have poverty consciousness.

Alternatively you could be very rich with a large bank balance and still have poverty consciousness. You could hoard your possessions and not enjoy or spend your money; always on the hunt for bargains and afraid to give too much away or to enjoy your money, a sort of 'Fagan'; your wardrobes cluttered with unused items. This could stop the flow of abundance as there is no circulation. Clearing out helps to bring abundance,' said Jo.

'There are laws which are universal, laws which are neutral regarding manifestation and we all have to abide by them whether we are selfish or kind. We can all have and create with cosmic energy if we know the way to go about it,' said Mariah.

Divine Abundance Stream

'So why are some not able to tap into the Divine abundance stream when they feel they are doing all the right things and yet struggling, and when on the other hand some people who might be greedy and controlling grow rich?' asked Jo.

'Well Jo, I understand that our thoughts would have to be a certain way and it does not matter whether we are spiritual or we are not spiritual or the way we live our lives, because the laws are still working,' replied Mariah.

'I know', if you look around you will see some people who have much wealth and are very powerful but you will notice that they have a vision and believe in themselves fully and that they can get anything they desire.

One way that they go about it is they first get skilled and carry on learning so they become expert in their ways. They use their energies and lots of time to make their dreams come true and do not for one moment take notice of any negative ideas from other people. They carry on aiming for their goals and draw to them people with similar ideas. Their sights are very firm in their thoughts every minute of the day. Yet on the other hand Mariah, some kind or spiritual people could have difficulty doing this, why is that?' asked Jo again.

Their secret

'Their secret is that we all send out a vibration or frequency as we mentioned earlier, and the vibration goes out and links up with a similar energy wave and draws or pulls towards us more of the same,' said Mariah.

'I understand we are an electromagnetic force field and we send out a vibration which goes and connects with comparable energy waves and then we draw to us more of this same energy, we attract this same energy.

For instance if we have been affirming night and day asking to be wealthy or any other desire and we are always talking about what we will do when we have the money because we really wish to have this money, and yet the money is still not coming to us. Why is that?' queried Jo once more.

'Because in our subconscious mind, for instance Jo, there could still old memories which say to us that we have to be a spiritual person or we must go without material things. We must forget about ourselves and think only of others, like a martyr, and if we remain spiritual then all will be provided to us, etc., etc. We forget that we are just as important and loving as the next person.

We change our minds and are not at all consistent or focused, we get excited one minute and think that we can do amazing things and then the next minute the doubts set in again. We say our abundance affirmations but then on the other hand we fret and concern ourselves about it all the time, about our bills or a better job with more money and we moan about paying the taxes, our rates or other every day concerns,' replied Jo.

'That's right Mariah, what we should be doing is focusing on the positive and having faith that we can do it or receive it. We should give blessings and gratitude when the money comes to us or what we have earned is exchanged for other people's services, there should be an exchange of energy,' said Jo.

'Some of us perhaps would not know what to do if we won the Lotto Jo, even if it seemed like a miracle to us. Some might hoard it for instance or become worried that it might be taken from them, which would be a shame because hoarding the money would then be useless to them,' continued Jo.

'On the other hand though they could spend it happily, have fun with it, make their dreams come true and also help other people to create their dream if they wished, because they would know that their abundance would keep on flowing and that their wishes and needs would always be met, they are thinking positive and happy.

As we said earlier it is up to the individual person whether the abundance would make them feel happy or not, because some very wealthy people are unhappy and bored with all their wealth; however they knew how to tap into the universal source by their desires, their thoughts and real determination and all the while they remained focused. They manifested because of their vision they always kept in front of them, their desire, their belief and actions and they would not be stopped in their endeavour,' said Mariah.

'So we could start to focus on all that we already have in our lives and give thanks for it. We could really stop and see and appreciate what we have and give thanks for it; be grateful. We could be joyful for all the good that we have in our lives and see and appreciate all the beauty around us and the kind smile or word that someone may have shown us today, or those that look out for us.

Instead of thinking about things that we think are wrong with us or surrounding us, we should see the beauty and the goodness, because if we act—not to squander foolishly—but act as if all this abundance and beauty from the universe is ours and is coming in a constant stream, then it will start to happen. Though enjoy that which is here for us right now, all the gifts,' said Jo.

'Sometimes our minds and thoughts are like a continuous record, playing over and over again our doubts and fears, or that we feel guilty over something and sometimes very negative. This would cancel out any of the wonderful affirmations that we may have been concentrating on to bring about our abundance.

Some days we may think that our dreams will come true and another day unfortunately we may feel very doubtful about ourselves or feel full of self pity, so once we realise that we are doing this we could quickly change our thoughts to the more positive thoughts of that which we wish to focus on to bring about our abundance.

So, even if we are very spiritual but we do not take advantage of the abundance stream with our mental mind and our mental body which would allow us to bring the manifestation energies, then while we are here on Mother Earth we will not be able to be a co-creator of abundance,' continued Jo.

'Remind me again Jo, how to do all this?' asked Maria.

"Well Mariah, the same as when we are asking the Angels, we should make it clear what we choose to manifest and feel it strongly in our heart.

Next we should ensure that our desires are in tune with our higher-self. We should ask that it be for the highest good for others and for ourselves because we cannot always see how things will turn out in the long run.

We don't want our dreams to be limited by our human desires alone as there could be a larger and more beautiful picture than we can visualise right now. We could listen to our intuition, our inner self; the inner voice that we may hear in our quiet moments or the feelings that nudge us.

We can listen for any guidance and then go with our feelings, act upon them and expect a miracle. If we should become doubtful or our ego takes over and we should feel we are not worthy or any other negative feelings for instance, then transmute those feelings or thoughts and instead focus on our dream again,' said Jo.

'Also by being thankful and grateful for all the little things that take place along the way, this brings about bigger gifts for us.

When we think as much as we can on the positive side we are bringing more of the positive to us. We are making a force field of abundance and love and no one can take away this harmony from us, only we can do that which we would not want to.

And the secret is that the more we are aware of and look for this spiritual harmony, our abundance will bring us great happiness because we are in the stream of creation and in harmony with Universal Law,' continued Jo.

'So, we should see the vision of our path strongly and of our dreams, and not let any one stand in our way of this, even though it might not be easy to overcome our old built up habits and thoughts over very many years.

Dream big and reach for the stars and remember that we will experience those things that we create with our thoughts, so let's once more as in the previous Golden Ages, create a beautiful paradise on earth with love and harmony.

Things are now changing and we are evolving with the coming of the new Golden Age, we are going back to our perfect state of joy and harmony and our beauty will shine brightly,' Mariah responded tentatively.

THE END

Books written by Colleen Costello:

'The Little Bright Lights—Mariah and Jo in Lemuria' . . . .
Published by Balboa Press

'Who We Are' . . . . **Published by Balboa Press**

To be published . . . .

'The Little Bright Lights—Mariah and Jo in Atlantis

'The Little Bright Lights—Mariah and Jo and the Angelics'

'The Little Bright Lights—Mariah and Jo and the Galactics'

'The Little Bright Lights—Mariah and Jo on Native American Lands'

'The Little Bright Lights—Mariah and Joe—The New Golden Age

'The Little Bright Lights—Mariah and Jo—Create your World